UNLIKELY PILGRIM

A JOURNEY INTO HISTORY AND FAITH

ALFRED S. REGNERY

BEAUFORT
BOOKS

UNLIKELY PILGRIM

Library of Congress Cataloging-in-Publication Data
Names: Regnery, Alfred S., 1942- author.
Title: Unlikely pilgrim / by Alfred S. Regnery.
Description: First edition. | New York, NY : Beaufort Books, [2019]
Identifiers: LCCN 2018045112 | ISBN 9780825308871 (hardcover : alk. paper)
Subjects: LCSH: Christian pilgrims and pilgrimages. | Regnery, Alfred S.,
    1942---Travel.
Classification: LCC BV5067 .R44 2019 | DDC 263/.041--dc23
LC record available at https://lccn.loc.gov/2018045112

For inquiries about volume orders, please contact:

Beaufort Books
27 West 20th Street,
Suite 1102
New York, NY 10011
sales@beaufortbooks.com

Published in the United States by Beaufort Books
www.beaufortbooks.com

Distributed by Midpoint Trade Books
www.midpointtrade.com

Printed in the United States of America

Book designed by Mark Karis
Cover and interior illustrations by Geneva Welch
Cover Photograph by Jose Carlos Macouzet Espinosa

To Audrey, with much love.

CONTENTS

The Author walking in Italy

INTRODUCTION

OVER THE COURSE OF SOME TWENTY YEARS, a friend and I took eleven pilgrimages to the Balkans, Western and Eastern Europe, and the Middle East. This is the story of those trips. Each was relatively unplanned; most involved physically challenging travel, often along paths American tourists rarely tread. We did not set out to take a series of pilgrimages. Rather, we first took one trip together, to Mount Athos in Greece, and then another and another until it became clear that all these journeys together added up to what could be called pilgrimages.

The inspiration for choosing our destinations would develop from something in the news or a book one of us was reading, or even a chance conversation with somebody who had been there. We would do some research, reading about the location and exchanging thoughts on it. We would get a history or guidebook about the place and off we would go, usually on the fly, with little more than a reservation for the first night. But as it turned out, these series of pilgrimages made up an almost seamless web of travel into places that at first sight would appear to be disconnected but which in fact had significant historical and religious associations. The end result was a journey into the history of Christianity and Western civilization, and into the faith that emanated from them.

And what history and faith we encountered! We stayed in 1500-year-old monasteries, walked on Roman roads where St. Paul and his entourage had trod, biked on mountain trails in post-communist Eastern Europe, and followed paths millions of medieval pilgrims had trekked to the great pilgrimage destinations of Christendom. We rarely knew where we would sleep or find our next meal, but we always found a bed, and never without finding a good meal first. We had long and engrossing conversations with monks, with peasants, with scholars, with artists, and ordinary people we met along the way—and with each other.

We walked hundreds of miles and bicycled thousands. We rode in horse-drawn farm wagons and behind tractors. We hitchhiked, we took trains, boats, and buses and we walked some more, and some more. We got lost, found our way, got lost again. Blisters, cuts and bruises, pulled muscles and shin splints, bug bites and wasp stings were constants, but despite busy and dangerous roads, steep trails, shady characters and questionable-looking cheap hotels, we experienced no permanent injuries or even really bad experiences.

I could probably be called a Washington insider and, by some, even a D.C. swamp dweller. I have spent nearly forty years living in and around the capital city, worked in the highest levels of the federal government, participated in meetings and negotiations with national and international leaders, and have been invited to the best parties, dinners, and embassies. I have known political and business leaders of every stripe. I have appeared and written for many of the nation's leading media outlets, have published hundreds of books and as many bestsellers as about anybody in the publishing industry, and written a couple in addition to this one. But in many ways, these pilgrimages and the places I have visited have outshined all of those fancy people and places and made most seem insignificant in comparison.

Nick, my travelling companion, who wishes to remain at least partially anonymous, has had a different career, but one just as varied, as interesting, and as sophisticated—maybe more so; his path was in academia and in the diplomatic world, in government, and in ecclesiastical circles in the U.S., in Great Britain and around the world. As we travelled, we had an ongoing, never-ending conversation about our mutual experiences and impressions of the world—always interesting, always friendly, and always somehow related to where we were, who we saw, and what we were experiencing at the moment. A few of those conversations are repeated in this book, but most are not.

What we saw and learned on these trips almost boggles the mind. Nick and I are both well-educated and well-read, and before these trips we both knew a good deal about Greece and Rome, about medieval times, about the development of culture and religion throughout history, and about Europe, the Balkans and the Middle East. And we had both travelled extensively. And yet, despite our book knowledge and prior globetrotting, to actually visit places that we had only read about—and plenty that we had not—to talk to hundreds of people, to stay in their houses, monasteries, old castles and both luxurious and cheap hotels and hostels, provided an incomparable lesson of faith, of history, of culture and even of current affairs and politics and of the people responsible for it.

Paramount among the discoveries we made on these pilgrimages is the recognition that Christianity and Western Civilization are inalterably intertwined. Oh, we both knew that long before we embarked on these pilgrimages. But that recognition was solidified again and again, virtually everywhere we went, whether we were looking for Christian sites or not. Everywhere we went we found evidence of the Christian world, whether from the earliest days of the Church, from medieval times, or from the turmoil of the twentieth century. We visited the oldest surviving Christian church in the world, went to villages in Syria where the people still speak Aramaic, the language spoken by Christ. We sat in ruins of Roman buildings where St. Paul had established the first church in Europe. We visited the remains of the Seven Churches in Turkey to which St. John the Evangelist wrote letters which appear at the beginning of the Book of Revelation. We sat on a stone wall overlooking the site where the Emperor Constantine oversaw the hammering out of the Nicene Creed—the negotiation that saved the Roman Empire, for awhile at least, which established once and for all that Jesus Christ was God, and which resulted in Christianity being adopted lock, stock, and barrel by the Romans. We saw dozens—perhaps hundreds—of Greek and Roman ruins, some from hundreds of years B.C., others from the time of Christ or afterwards. These ancient architectural remains still showed the massive strength and prowess of Greco-Roman culture and empire, which was eventually conquered by an idea, a set of principles, a religion. We saw remnants of the Middle Ages from all sorts of perspectives—from the monasteries in half a dozen countries, to the pilgrim trails winding their way through Western Europe to Rome and to Santiago de Compostela. It was eye-opening to walk along those pathways once trod upon by millions of medieval pilgrims and imagine that we were, ourselves, there to do penance in the fourteenth century.

I had come back to Christianity shortly before the first of these trips—I was raised in a Christian family, but had drifted away during my formative years—and later, sometime in the middle of these pilgrimages, had left the Episcopal Church and become a Catholic. No doubt visiting some of the great old Christian spots in the world, places where Christianity and particularly Catholicism had thrived and been hugely influential, and seeing their liturgies up close and actually participating in them, had an impact on my journey into Catholicism. As I sorted out all these experiences in my mind, I gained not only the historical perspective of it all but a foundation on which to better understand the part that the Catholic Church plays in modern times.

Each trip was unique, but when recalled together, as I have tried to do here, they became an overwhelming lesson in the impact of Christianity on the ways and people of the world. It is my hope that some readers may be sufficiently inspired that they, too, will follow in at least a few of these footsteps. If not, I should hope that I might stimulate, in readers minds, even a vicarious and imaginary pilgrimage or two.

1

MOUNT ATHOS, GREECE

June 1996

AS I LEFT WASHINGTON FOR GREECE in June of 1996, my eighty-three-year-old father—probably the most important person in my life—lay in a coma, near death, in a hospital in Chicago. I debated cancelling the trip but a priest, and a great friend, urged me to go. God, he said, would care for my father.

My travelling companions were my old British friend Nick, who I first met when he was studying in the US and who had subsequently received his PhD in theology in England, and Wolfgang, a German neurologist who was the father of a German exchange student who had stayed with us for a year. While I was visiting him in Munich several months earlier, he told me about previous visits to Athos, said he was planning to go again, and wondered if I might like to come along. Nick and I had become good friends playing Beethoven string quartets together—he a violinist, I a violist. He seemed like an ideal companion for such a trip, as he turned out to be.

I had joined the Episcopal Church several years earlier and was becoming interested in the history of Christianity, and thought that a trip to such a place as Mt. Athos would be both fun and educational. Raised in a Quaker family, I had never been baptized, and in fact Christianity was at best an afterthought for much of my life until then. Or at least until, one Christmas morning a couple of years earlier, I was reading a collection of writings by Aleksandr Solzhenitsyn which my company had just published, in which he described the pogroms, violence, and killings that went on in Russia in the early Communist days after World War I. Solzhenitsyn recounted the story of an elderly man in a small village who was asked how such things could happen in the world. His reply: these people have forgotten God. This is what happens when God is no longer the defining influence in one's life. As I read the passage, it was as if somebody had struck me in the face. As I asked myself whether I was forgetting God, I jolted into realizing that I was, in fact a Christian and decided to do something about it. I approached my friend Nick, who was then a seminary student who lived near us, and we soon were spending hours together reading and discussing the Gospels.

That June, we spent a week on Mount Athos walking some 160 kilometers or so from monastery to monastery over rocky, untravelled terrain, visiting the churches, talking to the monks, eating their food, sleeping in their guest rooms, absorbing their culture and, most of all, observing and admiring their faith in God. For this new Christian, it was a formative and profoundly moving experience of unchanged, living Christianity. I felt as if I had been transported centuries back into a medieval world. This beautiful and exalted spot nudges aside modernity in serene confidence, having spanned the turmoil of the past thousand years in unruffled contemplation of God.

The Greeks have various stories about the Holy Mountain, or Mt. Athos to the rest of the world. They tell how this cradle of Eastern Orthodoxy came to be where it is; how it is the way it is; how it became the Holy Mountain; and, most importantly, how the Mother of God became its celestial patron and protectress. One story known to all in the region relates that the Virgin Mary, accompanied by John the Evangelist, was en route to Cyprus by ship to visit Lazarus when they were blown ashore onto a peninsula by a violent wind. A voice said to them: "Let this place be your inheritance and your garden, a paradise and a haven of salvation for those seeking to be saved." And so it came to be.

Mount Athos is a haven, a tradition, and a living legend. The only inhabitants are Eastern Orthodox monks and a few hermits; the only buildings monasteries, several dating from the tenth century, others from the Middle Ages. They sit on a peninsula, about fifty kilometers long and eight or so kilometers wide, sticking down into the Aegean Sea in northeastern Greece. Flat at the edges, the land rises in clusters of increasingly high and rough mountains ending at the tip, the mountain Athos, its cliffs and bare slopes rising two thousand meters above the ocean.

The monasteries once flourished but have declined in recent years. Before World War I, the island had thirty thousand monks; there are now roughly two thousand—many monasteries are reduced to ten or twenty monks apiece. Panteleimonos, a huge Russian monastery which had three thousand monks in 1917, sits on its promontory in splendid loneliness, now all but empty.

Waiting for the Boat to Mount Athos, Ouranoupolis, Greece

Athos is a difficult and time-consuming place to reach. I met Nick and Wolfgang in Thessaloniki, a busy industrial city on the Aegean coast; the next afternoon, government bureaucrats ushered us into a spacious office in a drab building and issued us permits to enter the Holy Mountain. The Mt. Athos Pilgrim's Bureau allows only five non-Orthodox men to enter per day, and then only if they have applied weeks before. A letter of recommendation, attesting to one's moral character from a religious leader, is also required—preferably an Orthodox priest, but a Catholic or protestant clergyman will do. The office was only open for a few hours a day, and not until after the last bus had departed for the port where we would catch a boat to Athos. So after another day in Thessaloniki, we took a five-hour bus trip to the port of Ouronopolis (translated as the Kingdom of Heaven), a sun-drenched little village on the shore of the Aegean, the departure point of the only boats going to Athos.

Ouronopolis looked like something out of National Geographic. Near the shore, a large sign states in several languages and in no uncertain terms: "The entrance of women, the approach of crafts without a special permit, the stay of persons without a stay permit, any of the above involves serious penal sanctions." (American feminists lay down your placards and swords; the rule against women has been in effect since at least the ninth century and isn't likely to change without an order from on high.)

After our last set of papers was issued in a neat little white office on the dock, we embarked on our way to Athos. The boat carried a dozen or so monks, a couple of Frenchmen and Germans, forty or fifty Greek peasants and workers, two donkeys and the three of us. We spent about three hours on the azure blue of the Aegean, watching mountains in the background and a few other boats here and there, until we disembarked at the Xenophontos Monastery. We walked across a rocky shore and under ancient arched doorway of the monastery, up a gentle stone staircase, and into a courtyard surrounded by stone buildings and wooden balconies, trees, flowers, and fountains bathed in bright sun.

We entered a simple room overlooking the Aegean, where we were greeted by a handsome man of some thirty-five years, clothed in a long black habit and sandals, beard halfway down his chest, and hair gathered into a little ponytail. He brought us each a glass of cold water, a shot of ouzo, a piece of Greek candy, and a demitasse of strong and sweet Greek coffee. Soon we were shown to our room—a simple place with five or six steel cots and an open window overlooking the sea—and given the day's schedule.

After several days travelling halfway around the world by air, overnight in grimy Thessaloniki, a five-hour bus ride and the little boat, this austere, whitewashed room and the deep blue sea and sky outside the window suggested complete tranquility. I was overcome with a sense of peace, having finally safely arrived at this remote corner of Europe. Here was a place where, unlike Solzhenitsyn's village in Soviet Russia, the people had not forgotten God. God was the reason these men were here. As we would realize over the next several days, God had not been forgotten. God was here.

We changed into long-sleeved shirts—short pants are strictly forbidden and short sleeves frowned upon in church—and filed into the church for an hour-long Mass, all chanted in Greek, of course, and no different from the Mass of 500 years ago. The monks spend from four until eight o'clock in church each morning, and attend at least two other lengthy services daily. Special feast-day services may last for seven hours, from nine in the evening till four the next morning. The monks describe prayer as their job—that is why they are there—and the services, as one of them told me, are never boring, each being distinct from the others. After years of praying the services, the monks find that the church is their spiritual home, the place where they are most comfortable.

Supper was served immediately after vespers. The walls of the refectory were covered with sixteenth-century frescoes; the well-worn wooden tables long and low with benches along the sides, the sun shining through medieval windows in long soft rays. The monks sat at their tables, the pilgrims theirs. After a blessing, all sat down to metal bowls of vegetables or beans, freshly baked bread set in large baskets along the tables, with fresh cucumbers and Greek olives. The main course was a sort of stew made from spinach, onions, and a smattering of rice, no meat. A rough, homemade red wine was poured from a metal pitcher into tin cups. The monks raise almost all of their own food, tending their gardens as part of their daily work. All was silent but for the monotonous drone in Greek of the monk chosen to read a passage from the Bible. There would be no more food that day, and we realized we had better eat it all. And we had better eat it fast, for in ten minutes the abbot banged on the table with a little mallet, everyone stood, another blessing was given for the food consumed, and we filed out. After another thirty-minute Mass, the monks were free until 4 a.m.

Xenophontos was established in the tenth century, as were many of the monasteries on Athos; some were rebuilt after being destroyed by fire in the early nineteenth century, but parts of the old monastery, including the original church, remain. Orthodox monks, with their long beards, black square hats, and long robes, give the impression of being in another world. We were thus surprised by their easygoing and accessible manner, particularly one, who introduced himself as one of only two Americans on Mt. Athos.

Damianos, as he was called, was a doctor, about forty-five, to whom Wolfgang had become a sort of medical mentor. Dark with a chiseled face and a ponytail, a beard halfway down his chest, and sturdy arms and legs, he appeared to be a self-confident and self-reliant fellow. He grew up in a Greek family in Queens, New York, he told me, and when he could not get into an American medical school, took a crash course in Greek and entered Thessaloniki's medical school. He returned to New York for his residency, but found medical practice not to his liking and decided to become a monk. He had his own clinic in a quiet corner of the monastery, with two beds, an examination table, some relatively modern equipment, and a well-stocked pharmacy. Wolfgang had brought him a modern German X-Ray machine, the parts for which we had divided up before leaving Munich. His practice included visits to nearby monasteries to care for their sick, since most have no doctor. But, he explained, with little stress, a healthy diet, plenty of exercise and sunshine, and God very much a part of their lives, monks rarely get sick.

"From practicing medicine in New York to life as a monk on Mt. Athos is a long way," I remarked. "What possessed you to make such a change?" He had visited the Athos monasteries several times when he was in medical school, he told me, staying for a couple of weeks at a time. "I was intrigued by the life these men lived," he said. "In a world where faith in God was becoming an afterthought, the devotion that these monks reflected was palpable, and I found it inspiring."

I asked him whether he found any connection between what he saw in the monasteries and what he was studying in medical school at the time. "Good question," Damianos replied. "It had a great deal to do with it. As I studied anatomy and learned how the human body was made, how the different systems related to each other—in fact, the absolute mystery of humanity—the only explanation was God's plan and His exercise of that plan.

All of the science that the professors explained was fine, but it never went far enough to answer the hard questions of how all of this happened. The only answer, for me, was faith in God."

"So, when you decided to become a monk, what did you do?" I asked. "Did you just show up at the door and say you wanted to sign up?"

He laughed, answering that the process was long and involved. "The last things the monasteries want are people who come for a while, get bored or disenchanted, and leave," he said. "These places have been here for centuries, and they have survived through every kind of adverse situation. The Orthodox Church understands human nature, and it understands how to nurture the human spirit. If they didn't, the Church would have folded up centuries ago."

"So, then, what did you actually do?"

"First, I needed the blessing of the abbot to become a novice," he responded, "and after I received that, I moved to the monastery and started working in the gardens and the fields, cleaning the building, working in the kitchen. Hours and hours of strenuous work every day with the intention of wearing you down, designed to instill humility and remove temptations and to test your willingness to live this life every day until you die. You are giving yourself to the monastery and to God, so the monastery needs to be sure that is what you really want to do. And you have to know that, yourself."

I asked whether monasticism had met his expectations. "More than you can imagine," he replied.

"Serving God has no equal. All day, every day, I know that God is watching me, and I try to assure myself that everything I do is for Him. That strengthens my medical practice—and being one of the only doctors here reinforces that thought every day. But being a doctor is not all that I do. I work in the fields, I clean the monastery, work in the kitchen, and join the other daily tasks to keep this place going. And I talk to people like you about what I do and how I try to serve God."

"People like me? Pilgrims?" I asked.

"We show them how we live," he replied. "Many pilgrims come here because there is something discordant, wrong in their lives. If we can help with that God is pleased. Seeing that everything we do is for God may have some impact on them. And," he said as he smiled, "pilgrims are about the only contact we have with the outside world. We have no newspapers or radio or television. We very rarely leave. So talking to the pilgrims keeps us somewhat aware of what happens outside the Holy Mountain."

"You are pretty isolated here," I agreed. "But you probably don't experience much stress, and you spend hours every day in prayer. I wonder, then—what is your greatest challenge?"

"Pride," he replied.

"We monks must strive to maintain absolute humility. We must be totally subservient to God and to Christ. Everything we have comes from God, everything we believe comes from God, and everything we do is for God. If ever we should start thinking that perhaps we have some of the answers—well, once we lose our humility before God, all is lost."

I was stunned. Even in these monasteries—on a peninsula miles from the mainland, removed from the forces of the modern world, without communication, having only the barest essentials, spending all waking hours in prayer or in hard physical labor—how was humility even a question?

Monks at Xenaphantos Monastery, Mount Athos, Greece

Damianos replied that it was as easy for a monk on Mt. Athos to lose his humility as for any other human being. "It's no different for us monks than it was for the monks here in the fifteenth and sixteenth centuries. It's no different for me than for any other human being anywhere in the world, no matter who they are," he said. "The same forces, the same threats are universal. They come from within, not from the outside world." Not much different, I mused, from what we all face.

I asked him about what problems he encountered when he decided to become a monk. "The transition from practicing medicine to monasticism isn't exactly moving from one office to another," I remarked.

"Yes," Damianos answered, "the greatest threat to my resolve was my family. They did everything in their power to discourage me from joining, convinced that the monastery was some sort of cult. But now," he continued, "they have accepted it and even visit me from time to time."

Nick asked him about his greatest anxiety. His faith, he said.

"To come to Athos, I had to give up everything: my career as a doctor, my family and friends, the thought of marriage, contact with women—all of which I did willingly." But should he lose his faith, where, he asked, would he go? What would he do? He could, of course, leave the monastery at will. But for where, and for what? On the other hand, without his faith, life in the monastery would be meaningless. How could one stay, he asked, without faith?

It was clear from talking to Damianos that theirs was an uncomplicated faith unchanged through the centuries. Life is taken at face value, reality is not questioned, and obedience to God is paramount.

As our long conversation came to end, I realized that what Damianos had told me was probably the most profound thing I had learned on the entire trip. I have recounted the conversation many times since. It explains, more than anything else I saw, read, or heard, what the life of an Athos monk is all about. Damianos had been from one end of Athos to the other and to all of the monasteries and many of the skitis—small outposts affiliated with a monastery where monks would go by themselves or with one or two others for additional isolation and contemplation. As we prepared to leave Xenophantos he suggested that our next stop should be Borogoditsa where, he said, we would find only one elderly monk. It would take much of a day to get there, he warned, so be prepared for a long and arduous walk.

Since our visit to Mt. Athos, I understand that the European Union has provided large quantities of money to improve the roads and trails; in 1996, the roads were rutted and rough, trails were often difficult to find and simply did not appear on the maps, and finding one's way was often difficult. But we were all experienced hikers, had a good compass and a hiker's altimeter and an accompanying contour map. Since Wolfgang had been to Athos several times, he knew how to navigate this difficult terrain, so Nick and I followed his lead as we set off along a road which eventually turned into a barely passable trail that looked as though nobody had been along it in weeks. It was a typical day of about ninety degrees, hot sun and little breeze, and a beautiful clear sky. Bogoroditsa lay somewhere ahead, but it was often difficult to find the trail and the map wasn't much help: New logging roads had been pushed through the woods and the terrain did not seem to match the maps. After several hours through thick underbrush, we suddenly saw towers and stone walls peeking up through the trees. We found one gate, locked from the inside, but nobody seemed to be there. We rang a bell attached to an old rope several times and waited. Again. And then again.

After ten minutes or so the door inched opened and out poked the head of an elderly monk. He invited us in; he spoke enough German for us to be able to converse. He was Russian, he told us, from Odessa, and came here in 1946. He was now alone. Once there were three hundred monks at the monastery, although in his lifetime only eighty at the most. All had died but our new friend.

He asked us to sit on a bench overlooking a badly overgrown courtyard. The grass had not been cut in years; grapevines had spread everywhere. The buildings were in disrepair, a haunted ghost-town air about them. He brought us each a glass of cold water and then slowly disappeared up an outside staircase. When he reappeared several minutes later, he had a plate with three biscuits, which he placed in front of us. He exuded kindness.

After a few minutes he took us to the kitchen. It was dark, with a large wood-fired stove and an equally large wooden table with a sixteenth-century look to it. A few melons and various vegetables sat around, along with a jar of pickles and a bag of dried beans. The refectory, covered with frescoes and filled with long tables, could seat a couple hundred people, but today serves only this lonely monk.

The church was full of icons and more frescoes, the other rooms replete with pictures, old furniture, and candlesticks collected over hundreds of years. He was quick to shut the outer door—to "keep out the snakes," he warned us. Finally he took us to his sitting room and proudly showed us what must have been one of his most prized possessions—a painting of Czar Nicholas II and his czarina. I wondered for a moment if he realized that the czar had been dead for almost eighty years.

The old monk was alone but did not seem to be lonely; his

fellow monks may have been gone, but in a sense, they were still there, as were the saints painted on the icons and, of course, Jesus Christ, whose presence was universal. As Damianos had made so clear, the monks were here not for companionship but to serve God, and God would take care of them—or, in this case, take care of him alone.

After several hours, we walked on to Simonos Petras, one of the largest and most famous monasteries, built on a cliff high above the sea, a veritable fortress, with balconies clinging to the upper parts of the building. The structure looked, from a distance, as if it had been built there by a swarm of bees or insects. As we got closer, it took on a more human appearance. The building had burned down several times, most recently in 1895, but was always rebuilt somewhat different than the original structure, so it lacked any symmetry.

Here I met Ambrosia, the only other doctor on Mt. Athos, who trained in Germany and was an old friend of Wolfgang's; he took responsibility for us as his special guests, escorted to the best room in the monastery, generally reserved for VIP guests (which in his eyes we were), and allowed to use the bathroom with hot showers—the first we had experienced in several days. After vespers and supper, we were given a tour of the monastery: first the doctor's offices and pharmacy, then the various work rooms and kitchen, and then the church.

Of special interest was an amazing woodworking shop, presided over by Brother Ambrosia and outfitted with the latest German power equipment. Here the monks made furniture for the monastery, repaired doors and windows, and structured paneling for remodeling jobs. Ambrosia was enormously proud of the shop.

One of the monks was an electrical engineer who had built a modern and powerful electrical generating system powered by a waterfall, which was used for heat, the woodworking machinery, and various other jobs. This small link with the twentieth century seemed incongruous, since otherwise Simonos Petras was as antiquated as all the other monasteries. Even with electricity, the life of the monks remained simple and in service to God.

But we learned that things were closer to modernity than life on the surface indicated. Ambrosia escorted us down into the bowels of the monastery, through massive locked steel doors, and into a library. Modern movable shelves, controlled temperature and humidity, and track lighting emulated the most modern university library.

I learned later that the libraries in Athos contain what is probably the best collection of medieval books in the world, and certainly many of those were in this modern library at Simonos Petras. Ambrosia and another monk showed us just a few of the monastery's treasures, including a handwritten and illustrated copy of the Book of John made here in the eleventh century; a children's book hand-drawn in the fourteenth century; Bibles illustrated with colored miniature drawings compiled through the ages, all perfectly preserved against rot and mold.

As we wended our way down the mountain the next morning, away from Simonos Petras, down a steep and twisting trail worn into the land over hundreds of years, we looked back to see Ambrosia leaning over the balcony waving at us—a small and lonely figure, pleased to have had visitors, but ready to recede back into monasticism, into contemplation of and communion with God and Jesus Christ. Their hope and prayer was that our brief visit would enhance our Christianity.

Only ten outsiders are allowed onto the Holy Mountain a day, and, probably to minimize Western influence, only three of those may be nonmembers of the Orthodox Church; visits are typically limited to four days. For me, a relatively recently converted Christian, to be one of those three, and to have spent eight, instead of four days there, was a blessing.

When Mary and St. John arrived at Mt. Athos, the Greeks say that God told her it would be a "haven for those who seek salvation." Athos is indeed a haven and a paradise of peace and tranquility—starkly beautiful, with its long, unchanged Mediterranean coastline, vast virgin forests, and few roads or other developments except for the monasteries and their little skitis scattered about the peninsula.

But this haven, this sanctuary, was not merely the place itself; it is the monks and their simple life, unchanged since the Middle Ages, dedicated to serving God all day, every day, for a lifetime. Since that visit I have thought many times about their devotion to their faith and to God, and how they play a small but important role in the Christian world, anchoring centuries of Christianity by their longevity, their prayer, and their very presence in the world.

I called my mother when we landed in Munich to learn that my father had died that morning. God had taken care of him as the priest had predicted.

Any doubts I might have had about the role God plays in our lives had ended as Nick, Wolfgang and I made our way across this holy place and visited with these holy monks. I was fully aware that my father, too, was now free from the ties of this world and had found his place in eternity.

2

ON THE CAMINO DE SANTIAGO DE COMPOSTELA, SPAIN

June 1997

IN JUNE OF 1997, after a fast trip on the TGV from Paris, I sat in a café outside of the station in Bayonne waiting for Nick to arrive from London. I had met good friends the evening before in Paris for a long and leisurely dinner in a little restaurant—friends who were now Americans but who had come from Budapest at the time of the 1956 uprising there, escaped through the clutches of the Russians into Austria soon before the gates clanged shut again, and who, now in their sixties, still lived their lives as if every minute was a blessing from God. Now I was waiting to join Nick on another pilgrimage that I hoped would also be a blessing—the famous Camino de Santiago de Compostela in Spain.

Countless millions of pilgrims have made their way to

Santiago de Compostela in the northwestern most corner of Spain. As Rome became more and more of a cesspool in the Middle Ages, Santiago, the site of the burial of Saint James, became the principal pilgrimage destination in all of Europe. Trails led there from Eastern Germany and Poland, from Italy, Paris, and Canterbury and even from the Holy Land. St. Francis of Assisi went there not once but twice—over 2000 kilometers each way, all on foot in what we would consider unimaginable circumstances. In the literature of pilgrimages, Santiago de Compostela is always at the top, or very close to the top, of the list. The Spanish Camino leads from the French border, near the Atlantic and the port of Bayonne, across Northern Spain to the ancient city of Santiago, and is as well travelled as any pilgrimage way in the world. It is, according to James Michener, the finest journey in Spain and one of the two or three best in the world. After Nick and I had walked from monastery to monastery on Mt. Athos, the Camino seemed like the next logical trek in what would become this twenty-year pilgrimage from political Washington to the peacefulness of the Christian world's great roads.

I had read several accounts of the Camino and knew it was going to be a grueling couple of weeks. I was in pretty good shape, had walked for miles and miles before leaving, carrying a pack full of bricks to strengthen my legs, but I was still worried that I had brought too much along, that I couldn't keep up, and would get terrible blisters or worse. But these worries were alleviated by learning what the original pilgrims—those poor wretches in the Middle Ages—went through, those who had no way to bail out if things got out of hand, who rarely had enough to eat, were at the mercy of highwaymen, thieves, thugs, every sort of con man, not to mention the weather and God knows what else.

And whatever doubts I had about stamina were overcome by the sense of relief I felt in getting away from Washington and into territory where I would be anonymous, where I would find a new world, and a place that was certainly one of the most holy places in Christendom. I had just been badly abused by poison-pen, hatchet-woman Jane Mayer, in a nasty profile in the *New Yorker* which was still ringing in my ears. That too, I told myself, would pass.

Nick was as glad to be there as I was and over a leisurely glass of beer, we compared notes about what to expect on the trip as well as what had been going on in our lives since we had last met. We compared the various books about the Camino that we brought along as we rode a little train up the mountain into the Pyrenees to St. Jean Pied de Port, the traditional starting point of the Spanish Camino de Santiago.

The little town looks the part with crooked cobblestone streets, medieval walls, and a fortress with a partially destroyed tower keeping watch over it. Our first stop was at the official pilgrim's office, a little stone house where we were welcomed by a middle aged woman who obligingly gave us our passports—a document with places for stamps at each overnight stop which must be stamped by a monk or public official. When the passport is full upon arrival in Santiago, one is declared a true pilgrim and given a diploma at the Cathedral.

Pilgrims' passports in hand, we went to the Refugio, an overnight lodging of sorts only for pilgrims. But the place was already full—all six beds taken—so we headed on to a pension (a sort-of European boarding house) in the center of the village and were given a couple of tiny rooms, mine with no window or other ventilation. The fare was demi-pension, which meant it included supper. Many of the guests, unlike us, had been walking all day and were ready for a filling meal. The menu was plat du jour, whether you liked it or not, and reassured us that we would not go hungry. First came a great bowl of spaghetti with a tasty and filling sauce, followed by a platter with five lamb chops for each diner, complete with French fries, salad, and dessert with the obligatory coffee and a bottle of wine.

Our first day was simply magnificent. We were up before six and, after an early breakfast, walked out of St. Jean and up a steep, S-curved gravel road into snow-peaked mountains. We were alone—no traffic, no other walkers, just the view across the Pyrenees into Spain. From time to time we would see shepherds with their herds and their dogs, and a few cows and horses. As we went higher, we were struck by the fierce, cold winds—winds so strong that it was almost impossible to walk, reminding us of the millions of feet that had preceded us over the centuries. But we each had modern backpacks, plenty of water and a full stomach, comfortable hiking shoes and high-tech windbreakers. We wondered what those poor souls went through who had come along here 500 years earlier—wearing, no doubt, heavy sandals and carrying what they could but relying on others for their food and drink and a place to sleep. Their motivation was faith, love of God, and a belief that making their way along this Camino to the shrine of St. James would, if they survived the journey, facilitate their entry into heaven.

St. James was Jesus' first cousin, the brother of John. Salome, their mother, the cousin of the Virgin Mary, married to the Galilee fisherman Zebedee. The brothers were Jesus' most devoted and enthusiastic disciples, two of the earliest to be chosen. Both were present when Jesus was crucified, and James, in the year 44 AD, was beheaded by order of King Herod of Agrippa. Tradition holds, and it is suggested in the Book of Acts, that after the Resurrection the disciples scattered to various distant lands to proselytize. James went to Spain, where he converted nine Iberians to Christianity before returning home to his native land.

There is a legend, widely believed and often told by Spaniards, that James's body, his head mysteriously reconnected, turned up in the Spanish port of Jaffa on a stone boat manned by knights. His body was brought to the harbor of Padron, on Spain's Western coast, and was buried in a Roman burial ground. The legend holds that in the year 814—eight centuries later—a hermit spotted a bright star which led him to St. James' burial place. The body was disinterred, still completely intact. Further legends claim that a resurrected St. James then led Christians battling the Muslims who had overrun the Spanish peninsula. Riding a great white horse, he killed thousands of Moors so that the Christians reclaimed Spain as their own. St. James—Santiago Matamoros, as he was known—became the patron saint of Spain and was buried in Santiago de Compostela, which in turn became the most holy place in Iberia and the destination of choice for millions of pilgrims. Historians estimate that as many as half a million people a year, for roughly one thousand years made the pilgrimage.

After twenty kilometers or so we came to the top of the pass. It was bleak, cold, the winds continuing to howl, and as desolate as Scotland in the winter. We walked along a barbed wire fence marking the border between France and Spain and down into a forest of huge beech trees. Suddenly the wind was gone, the sun shining as if we had suddenly passed from Northern to Southern Europe.

And indeed we had. We made our way to our first overnight stop, the ancient castle at Roncesvalles, often said to be where Spain begins, and the site where Charlemagne was defeated by the Basques in 778.

From Roncesvalles we did something very un-pilgrim like but, under our circumstances and the time constraints imposed by modern-day Washington and London and the rest, was necessary: We took buses, jumping ahead through Pamplona, home of the famous running of the bulls, to Burgos, provincial capital of Castile, home to many Medieval churches, including the Cathedral of St. Mary, and ultimately to Leon, site of one of the great cathedrals in Spain, and our next stop.

Many of Northern Spain's churches are Romanesque, the architectural period preceding Gothic, built between about 1000 and 1400 AD. They are a less complicated style than Gothic, without the frills, the little towers and many stone carvings that dominate Gothic churches. But Leon's churches are early Gothic, and by and large resemble Romanesque style. Leon's Cathedral is especially noteworthy for its glass windows; it is believed that it has more square meters of glass than of stone—an unimaginable feat when one considers the engineering and architectural sophistication that must have existed in the fifteenth century. It has 125 large windows—most cathedrals may have a dozen or so—plus fifty-seven round windows and three huge roses, all of stained glass, much of it the original stuff. Leon is known as the Cathedral of Light, but only in recent years, with the advent of modern lighting, has its magnificence become known.

When it was built, and for all but the last several decades, the stained glass could only be seen from the inside, and then only on a bright day. Little did we realize what a treat we were in for. "Come back after the sun goes down," a priest with whom we had struck up a conversation told us in surprisingly good English, "and you will see something the builders of this church could never have imagined." By simply throwing a switch, he told us, the church becomes brightly lit on the inside, and the stained glass reveals its full glory from the outside.

We returned after supper and were not disappointed: the stained glass windows were as alive from outside the church as they would be from the inside on a bright summer day. You have to wonder what the medieval architects and builders would have thought, and you cannot help but marvel at the skill they had to design and build an edifice that would someday demonstrate beauty far beyond anything they could imagine.

Leon is about halfway between St. Jean and Santiago. From here our transportation of choice, with the exception of a short hitchhike or two, and a ride on a horse drawn wagon, would be on foot. After we had left the Pyrenees, the countryside had been open plains, rolling and green and seemingly stretching on to the horizon. Beautiful country, indeed, but monotonous for walkers: each hour with the same scenery and each town about the same along the way. Had we been true pilgrims, of course, we wouldn't have a bus to catch, a car to flag down. But we were moderns, and just wanted to get a flavor of what had gone before.

Once we got underway we moved along at a decent pace, covering twenty-two kilometers in about five hours. The walk out of Leon seemed interminable, along a busy road with retail establishments, then small factories, junkyards, and finally into open country. Cars and trucks barreled down the highway at breakneck speeds as we trudged along the side—something that we would find all too common on the Camino. The highway passed through a couple of little villages, all but destroyed by the traffic, and into La Virgen del Camino, which had a rather modern Dominican church but included a baroque tower. The old church had been replaced, we were told, in the 1960s on the site of a church built in the sixteenth century; there is a legend that the Virgin appeared to a local shepherd, Alvar Simón, and asked him to hurl a stone with his sling and to see that a church be built where the stone landed.

As we rested our weary legs in the churchyard, Nick mentioned what a completely different experience this was from Mt. Athos—a theme we often came back to as we walked along. Athos, Nick thought, reflected the Orthodox way of life—closed to the outside world, except to a very few privileged people; structured in a completely top-down manner, stern and almost humorless, the monks leading a life they considered seamless with the life they would experience after death. The Camino, on the other hand, was more Catholic—open to all, alive, reflecting the life the people lived outside of the pilgrimage. Thousands, tens of thousands of pilgrims had been on this trail at any given time since about 1000 AD, each becoming part of the Camino, in a sense, and the Camino becoming part of them. The pilgrims encountered joy, pain, sorrow, hunger, cold or whatever might come along around the next corner. The Athos monks, on the other hand, lived in a separate world, where everything was controlled, with no surprises and virtually no outside influences.

Soon after leaving town, the trail broke off into the woods, and we were again away from the highway, walking through beautiful rolling land, along streams, through woods and an occasional village. Around one bend was a shepherd and a couple hundred sheep kept in the flock by a collie. What a thrill to watch this little dog, running from one side of the flock to the other, rounding up the sheep while his master looked on! A tall and kindly looking man with a great mustache, he sported an old felt hat, a long raincoat, and leather boots so well worn that they must have belonged to his grandfather. Pilgrims walking along the trail 500 years ago could have seen just the same man, with the same outfit, the same hat and almost the same boots, tending his sheep. Modernity probably had little impact on this fellow at all. Still a devout Christian; it was unlikely that he had ever been more than a hundred kilometers or so from his farm, and tending sheep was probably about the only job he knew how to do. Today's pilgrims, however, would be less likely to try to steal a sheep for dinner.

The scenery on the Camino changes constantly. Vast fields of grain give way to rolling hills set against mountains; the way is dotted with cities and, best of all, countless small villages, each with beautiful masonry—the stonework alone in the streets, walls, houses, and barns practically made the trip worthwhile. Everywhere we saw the most beautiful and carefully laid stonework, each stone perfectly fitted into the next, perfectly straight. Even barns and buildings abandoned decades before still stand straight and solid as could be. And the doors—wonderful wooden doors with well-fitted rails, often featuring carvings and applied designs, were to be seen on even the most insignificant buildings, barns, and sheds. The handwork, design, and proportion were all done to perfection.

The little peasant villages along the trail were also unchanged, in all likelihood, from the heyday of pilgrimages in the middle Ages. Cows and oxen passed us on the street, some pulling handmade four-wheel wooden wagons loaded high with hay on their way to the barn. Goats and chickens wandered about the road; children who looked like they could belong in any Mediterranean village, playing something like hopscotch, stopped to watch these two light-haired, blue eyed pilgrims walking through their town. But there was always a friendly-looking bodega, adorned with a red and white Coca-Cola sign and advertising various Spanish snacks and drinks. More often than not there would be a great tree spreading its shade in front, with a table and chairs underneath where a cold drink and a quick rest were most welcome.

Scallop shells on the road signs are the mark of the Camino—the trademark, if you will—and have been since at least the twelfth century. Since the shells are indigenous to the coast of Galicia in Spain, pilgrims would bring one home to prove that they actually made the trip to Santiago, using it, as they walked, as a drinking cup or small dish for food. Today, it marks The Way; at every turn, the shell is embedded in streets, in shop windows, and worn, in some image or other, by every pilgrim. It even shows up in fancy American restaurants as Coquille St. Jacques!

As the sun was sinking in the west we came to Villar de Mazarife, tired after twenty-one kilometers and ready for dinner and a comfortable bed. Following the shells and the signs, we came to the refugio—an old and decrepit-looking house, locked up tight as a barrel. But a sign pointed to the bodega a few doors down where, it said, we would find the key. A weathered woman in her sixties, dressed in a long black dress with a scarf around her head, who had no doubt seen every sort of creature making its way westward, gave us the key with strict instructions to return it in the morning. Unlocking the door, we found a room about fifteen feet square with several mattresses strewn about the floor. Down the hall was a small but clean bathroom with running hot and cold water—nothing fancy, but certainly all we needed.

Soon after we had begun to settle down for the night, the door opened and an exhausted Frenchman walked in.

He dropped his backpack and introduced himself as Henri—named, he told us, after his father who had died six months before. If he knew any language but French he wasn't going to admit it.

Henri was a colorful fellow, full of good cheer and plenty of conversation—only in French, of course. He was walking the Camino, he told us, to honor his late father. They had had an on-again-off-again relationship, at times bordering on mutual distrust and hatred and at others warm and loving, at least until something else

Pilgrim's Shell, Camino de Santiago, Spain

went awry. And something had gone awry sometime before his father's demise.

"I am not a particularly religious fellow," Henri explained. He was a Catholic in the modern French tradition of not being very Catholic, nor very devout about anything except perhaps being French. But after reading and pondering the Fifth Commandment he had decided that he should undo the dishonor and hurt he had caused his father by becoming a pilgrim to Santiago. He had started near Paris and had been underway for several weeks. "At every church, every shrine, every cross along the side of the road," Henri told us—and this was no trifling number—"I stopped, murmured a prayer, and asked God's forgiveness for the way I had mistreated the old man." We took Henri to dinner at Villar de Mazarife's only restaurant, where the conversation carried on over the plato del dia and a couple of bottles of local Rioja.

The next day we covered over forty kilometers with legs and feet that were beginning to feel like those of the millions who had gone before us. We walked through the little town of Hospital de Orbigo, ate our breakfast sitting on a fantastic Gothic bridge built in the thirteenth century, then shouldered our packs and headed on to Astorga, a Roman city with a great Romanesque church closed to the public, and an underground prison for slaves.

Since our trek in 1997 the Camino has moved into the twenty-first century. Many more people now do it, partially because of the popularity of the movie The Way, which gives quite an accurate portrayal. We would often go for miles without seeing anybody, and were often virtually the only guests in a refugio. But even more so than Hollywood, what has brought the greatest change is the internet. There were no cell phones in 1997; we were largely cut off from the world, and it was easy to begin to think we were real medieval pilgrims. Today, the refugios all advertise Wi-Fi connections, and everybody is electronically tied to the world.

But in between those stops, walking for hours on end, along paved roads through towns and villages, across vast plains, through the woods on well-worn paths, up and down rocky trails, even a modern walker would begin to feel just a little like the medieval pilgrims who day after day made their way to Santiago to pay tribute to the tomb of St. James. We certainly did. In a way, you begin to get into their heads, their bodies, their legs and feet, even their shoes. You think about what might have motivated them to make this distant journey across foreign lands, risking their health and well-being, their lives. You think of them setting off carrying whatever money they could scrape together and a few extra clothes in a leather bag slung over their shoulder. They came from France, Germany, and further east; from Italy and from England, and of course from all over Spain. Often they would be gone for a year or more, walking by day, staying in the equivalent of a refugio or, if they were lucky, in the occasional inn or farmhouse. Sometimes they would have to sleep in the open or under a cloth to protect them from the weather. You think of them getting a blister or a cut, and that turning into an infection or worse. No medical care, no first aid, no antiseptics or pain killers, just another mile of road ahead. You thought of the thieves and highwaymen, and the swindlers and charlatans, doing their best to take the pilgrims' money or valuables. You thought of the food they must have eaten: no nice bodega with a hot sausage or fresh sandwich and a cold

Coca-Cola, but scrounging what they could not buy, eating fruits, nuts, and berries when they were ripe, perhaps trapping or shooting a wild animal from time to time and cooking its meat alongside the road. And water? No bottles of clean, fresh spring water from Evian, just dirty water in streams, or an occasional drink from a well or a spring, more likely than not dirty, smelly, or polluted.

Some were not willing walkers but had been sentenced by a judge or a master as penance for some wrongdoing as an alternative to being thrown in a dungeon; community service medieval style. One story circulates of a poor German sentenced by a judge for murder to walk from Eastern Germany to Santiago and back carrying—and only a German could think up such a punishment—the corpse of the fellow he had murdered. Many of the pilgrims were not poor peasants but the elite, some travelling with an entourage, some in coaches or on horseback. Saints, kings, knights and tradesmen often walked or rode beside peasants, monks and priests, and even the destitute. The crowds of travellers were such that the earliest known guidebook is a guide to the pilgrimage to *Santiago: The Codex Calixtinus*, written in the twelfth century by Frenchman Aymeric Picaud, described the "French route"—the one we were on—telling of the villages, the terrain, the churches, monuments, and shrines, where inns were located, where food could be obtained, the quality of the water, the relics and sacred tombs open to visitors, and what was to be found upon arrival at Santiago and the St. James Cathedral.

And just who were all these people? The great storyteller Michener, in his book Iberia, describes seven different sorts of people. First were the devout Christians seeking salvation (and many of those, he says, being of ripe age, probably died along the way.) Second are knights who vowed to take the trip if they were successful in their battles, usually on horseback. Then there were monks, priests, and occasional cardinals for whom a visit to the tomb of a saint was the culmination of life in the Church. Fourth were criminals, sentenced by a judge to make the trek instead of serving time. Next were thieves, beggars and other unsavory characters who survived at the expense of the others. Sixth, says Michener, were tradesmen of every sort who sold or made whatever the hordes of pilgrims needed, and finally various government agents, keeping an eye out for whatever might be useful information for officials in Madrid.

For all stripes of pilgrim, there was also joy and happiness alongside the trials of the Camino. For some, a medieval pilgrimage was probably the equivalent to a modern vacation: See new places, meet new people. Be unrestrained by conventional rules and morals, have a good time, let it all hang out away from the prying eyes of nosey neighbors and village gossips. People would meet at an inn or over a meal, make friends, and walk on together. How many marriages, perhaps, came out of these pilgrimages—how many babies, how many shattered virginities?

But in the end the Camino was all about faith in God and belief in Jesus Christ. Nick had brought along a book with reflections on the Camino which we read from several times a day. It reminded us that to pilgrims nothing was more important; nothing could stand in the way of their dedication to their faith and their desire to exercise that faith by making a pilgrimage to a sacred place. Part of that faith was their conviction that heaven and hell were real places, and their actions on this earth would determine their ultimate fate. And so the perils that awaited them on the Camino were inconsequential as compared to the perils that awaited them if their souls were turned away from God.

Thinking on these things, we trekked onward, through a little village called Cacabelos and on to Villafranca, a medieval village virtually unchanged in 500 years, the crooked and narrow streets paved with cobblestones, worn smooth from the feet of the hordes of pilgrims who had passed through. The refugio was largely made from great plastic sheets as the building had burned down, but offered a family breakfast for weary travellers for less than $5.00. One of my most vivid recollections of that place was awakening in the early dawn to a recording of a Gregorian chant—among the purest and most sacred music that there is—and thinking for a brief moment that I must indeed have arrived in Heaven.

The next day we hiked up steep trails, along gravel roads, and through the virgin forests to a village perched on the top of a mountain called Carrero, the site of a miracle, according to legend, that made it one of the most sacred on the Way of St. James. One night, during a howling winter storm, as Mass was being sung to a few shepherds, a clap of lighting and thunder shot a bright light through the little chapel and on the altar the bread turned visibly into the Body of Christ and the wine in the chalice—the same chalice still used on the altar—became His blood. Then the voice of Jesus Christ was heard to say: "I too have come to hear Mass said this night, for I too am a shepherd."

I had developed the most astounding blisters on my feet, and my legs were so sore with what felt like shin splints that I could barely walk. I had hobbled into a drug store where the sympathetic pharmacist had provided various lotions and pills which helped the pain enough to continue on, slowly, but I knew the only cure was to stop walking. If there was one thing that bound me to the spirit of those millions of medieval pilgrims it was these shin splints—almost unbearable, unremitting and agonizing pain, but with no choice but to keep walking. Finally we did stop, at the top of that mountain, looking out for miles to the West, across a valley partially wooded and partially cloaked in great green fields. A flock of sheep, looking like a light cloud against the green grass, slowly moved along like one great animal.

Arriving in Santiago later that day (I had gone the last forty or so kilometers on the bus while Nick walked), still limping and somewhat bedraggled, I ambled into the lobby of the five-star Hostal de los Reyes Catolicos, one of Spain's Parador hotels, originally built by Ferdinand and Isabella around 1500 as a hospital and medical school—once considered the preeminent medical facility in the world and now the perfect place for a tired and sore pilgrim. Located just across the square from the Cathedral, it has seen more than a few pilgrims in far worse shape than I, and probably welcomed every one. Today it is one of the most sumptuous and comfortable hotels in Europe. They had an available room which I took immediately; as soon as I walked through the door, I slumped onto the bed, and shortly after was soaking in a hot bath, soothing my sore feet.

Santiago is dominated by the Cathedral, the central focus of the city square. It is one of the great shrines of all of Christendom: a monument to St. James, it has sheltered thousands of pilgrims since its construction in the eleventh century. Standing on the site of the original basilica built in the ninth century, its twin baroque towers are visible for miles away. It is unique, however, because there is not only one plaza in the front, but four—one on each side, all of which are architectural treasures. To the south is the Plaza de las Platerias (the Silversmith Plaza) a Romanesque square facing up to the bell tower, and where there is a statue of King David playing the violin. On the east side is a large and rather vacant square which extends out from the Holy Door of the Cathedral which is only opened in years of special pilgrimages and which is protected by statues of the twelve apostles, with a statue above of St. Athanasius and Santiago himself, outfitted in pilgrim's attire complete with floppy hat, a gourd and cockleshell—the very picture of a true Santiago pilgrim and a statue that remains in the memory for a lifetime.

Over a typical Galician dinner of boiled potatoes and cabbage alongside an unidentifiable cut of beef and, of course, a bottle of Rioja, Nick and I gathered together a few observations about the Camino that had occurred to us over the past days.

The Camino is alive and open, available to anybody who wants to travel on it for a day, for a month, a kilometer or the entire stretch to Santiago. For the past 1000 years it is estimated that half a million people a year walked the Camino. Each one made some small contribution, had left something, taken something along and in a sense, had become part of the legend that is the Camino de Santiago and the Camino had become part of them. Many, no doubt, had the most vivid experiences of their lives, whether by reinforcing or even finding their faith, giving birth to a child, watching a companion die, finding a good meal or going hungry for days at a time, finding a comfortable inn for the night or not finding one and sleeping along the trail. But once again it struck us that the overriding reason for making the trek was faith—faith in God and Jesus Christ. Without that there would be no Camino.

Cathedral at Santiago de Compostella, Spain

As we had discussed earlier, the Camino was so different from Mt. Athos. That place is closed to all but the privileged few, while the Camino is open to all. Athos is a restricted and controlled place, only inhabited by Orthodox monks and only visited by men who have been first cleared by the bureaucracy. On Athos there are no surprises, no outside influences and life is completely predictable. On the Camino there are as many outside influences, as many surprises, and as many distractions as there are people.

The Camino is a microcosm of life and of Christianity, made up of good people, thieves, murderers; some are there for the spiritualism, others for the sport of it. Some are celebrating a high in their lives, others trying to absolve some terrible pain. We saw bicyclists in Spandex, hippies in dirty rags, Germans in well-pressed Bavarian outfits as if they were walking right out of the sixteenth century, with long cloaks and floppy hats, their scallop shell hanging on a string around their necks. Each had his reason for the pilgrimage, but all were drawn by the attraction, the magnetism of the Camino de Santiago. All are driven to the same destination.

Experiencing that pull of the Camino firsthand had a profound effect on me. I was not yet a Catholic in 1997—I would join the Church five years later—but I cannot deny that I was interested in it. It didn't take long, after being baptized and joining the Episcopal Church, to feel that the Episcopal Church really didn't have much to offer. The central question, at least in the U.S., had to do with sexuality; I couldn't discern that the Episcopal Church stood for much of anything in that area. Even Nick, an Anglican theologian, admitted to me one day, as we walked along the Camino, that he sometimes felt like he was trapped on a sinking ship. Before going to Spain, I had struck up a dialogue with Fr. C. J. McCloskey, a Catholic priest famous for a string of conversions, who would bring me into the Church five years after the Spain trip. The miles I walked on the Camino brought me one step closer to finding my home in the Catholic Church.

Santiago de Compostela, James Michener writes, "is the very heart of the Church in Spain." If Santiago is the heart, the millions of pilgrims who walked the Camino are its soul. For me, even a few days on the Camino, shin splints and all, would leave a mark that I would not soon forget.

3

BICYCLING THROUGH NORMANDY AND BRITTANY

June 1999

I ARRIVED IN LONDON the day after my friend Jonathan Aitken was sentenced to eighteen months in prison for perjury and perverting the course of justice. The sentence screamed from the headline of every paper, the news desks of the television stations, and every other news outlet in Great Britain. Aitken was a member of Parliament, in John Major's cabinet, lived in Winston Churchill's old house around the corner from the House of Commons; he was a member of the Privy Council and had been often mentioned as the next prime minister. Because of his misdeeds, he lost his seat in Parliament, went bankrupt and lost his house, his wife left him, and he resigned from the Privy Council and went to prison. To say that he had taken a fall was an understatement.

This had no apparent relationship to the pilgrimage Nick and I were about to begin on that June day in London. Only later, after I had returned to Washington and after Jonathan had served his time did it all come together, and as I look back on it all, it was one more stone that solidified the foundation of my faith.

Aitken had always been a Christian—the sort of Christianity often practiced by well-heeled Englishmen. He was a member and warden of an Anglican congregation, but without taking anything too seriously, serving on many boards, giving his money to Christian charities. But when his life fell apart, things changed. He later told me, after he had been released, that when he was sentenced he was sent directly to the holding pen in the depths of London's famous Old Bailey, where he found himself surrounded by stinking drunks, thieves, gamblers, and male prostitutes. Terrified for his safety, and the subject of incessant intimidation by the other occupants of the cell, he discovered that in his pocket was a pamphlet entitled Praying the Psalms—a calendar booklet of daily readings that had been given to him earlier in the day. He flipped it open to June 8 to find Psalm 130 which begins,

Out of the depths, I cry to you, oh Lord,
Oh Lord, hear my voice,
Let your ears be attentive,
To my cry for mercy.

In an instant, he later told me, a sense of peace came over him, his terror was gone, and the obscenities of his cellmates obliterated. He knew that for the rest of his life he would be a dedicated and devout Christian, and indeed he remains one to this day.

I had come to know Aitken when we had published his award-winning biography of Richard Nixon several years earlier. Chuck Colson, Nixon's Special Counsel who went to prison during the Watergate scandal, had called me one day and urged me to look at Jonathan's Nixon manuscript. Colson had become a considerable figure in the evangelical community after becoming a Christian while in prison, and went on to found the Prison Fellowship. As I look back on that episode, I find it interesting that Colson, when he called me, had already become a Christian, but Jonathan had not yet, and of course time in prison was the furthest thing from his mind. Yet Colson had befriended him, recognized the merits in his book and was instrumental in getting it published. As Aitken later admitted, Colson was probably more of a reason for his conversion to Christianity than any other person.

Years later I saw Jonathan, after he got out of prison, from time to time in Washington or London. The way he managed to get through his fall and return to a productive life has always been a great inspiration to me, as it was to many others. He explained that although what he went through was more painful than anything he had ever imagined, after it was done he was not only a better person but had become totally dependent on God. Instead of reliance on money and political power he had found something else—something ultimately much more satisfactory and much more substantial. "Pride," he wrote in his memoir *Pride and Perjury*, "was the root cause of all my evils... If I had been blessed with a small helping of humility instead of possessed by a surfeit of pride, the entire tragedy would have been avoided."

No such hope for the future was yet on my mind as I had started off on a new pilgrimage in June of 1999. I had begun the day, fresh off the plane from Washington, at a bike shop on Gray's Inn Road where I bought a fine touring bicycle that would get me across France and presumably last for several years back in the States. I spent the better part of the day pedaling around London, visiting familiar sites and some new ones, and was reminded what a good way bicycling was to see a large, traffic-clogged city. But at every turn, as I would spot a newspaper for sale with Johnathan's name in 48-point type, and I was reminded of and saddened by his plight.

Late in the afternoon I met Nick at Waterloo Station, where we caught a train to Southampton and then an overnight ferry to Le Havre. The plan was to make a big circle through Normandy and Brittany, visiting cathedrals, monasteries, shrines, and other Christian sites, all the while enjoying this marvelous part of the world and getting plenty of exercise to boot, winding up in Paris ten days later. After the two long walking trips across the very Orthodox Mt. Athos and the very Catholic Camino de Santiago in Spain, a bicycle trip across civilized and secular France seemed like an interesting contrast.

While eating supper on the fantail of the ferry across the Channel, Nick and I talked about what he would be looking for on this pilgrimage. Nick remarked that although France had once been practically synonymous with Catholicism, the French had slowly abandoned most of their faith, starting with the Enlightenment and the French Revolution and progressing into faithless modernity. We wondered how much of the original spark still existed and we looked forward to learning what we could about the demise, firsthand, of Christianity in one of its former strongholds.

We covered about 100 km through lovely early summer

countryside the first day—a formidable ride, we concluded, for a couple of guys our age—and wound up at a comfortable bed and breakfast not far from Rouen. The owners sent us down the road to what they described as a "truck stop" for dinner, and to be sure, large trucks from various parts of Europe were in the parking lot and the place full of their drivers. This being France, the dinner was anything but greasy hamburgers and fries, but instead a homemade stew, fresh bread and salad, a decent bottle of local red wine all finished off with a fine piece of patisserie.

We arrived at the Benedictine Abbey at Bec just in time for Mass in the rectory, a beautiful building, the nave rather long and narrow but of the most perfect proportions. A choir was on hand, and it sounded as much like angels as anything I had ever heard. A group of twenty or so children participated in the Mass, adding a wonderful innocent dimension to it all. Nick mentioned that Bec was once a center for visits of Archbishops of Canterbury, and always maintained a strong British connection; famous Archbishop of Canterbury and martyr Thomas à Becket trained and lived there. It was badly damaged during the French Revolution, but was so well restored that what we saw could easily have been the original eleventh-century church.

Thirty or so white-robed monks were at the Mass; hard as we tried to engage with them, we had no luck. But an elderly man, seated on a park bench near where we had left our bicycles, asked whether we had been into the abbey and what our impression was. Bec, he told us, had been occupied by the French Army from when Napoleon closed it up in 1792 until after World War II, when it was reclaimed by the Benedictines and reopened. He told us he lived nearby, and came to the Abbey virtually every day to pray. "If God is not in this place," he said, "he is nowhere." There are six offices each day, he said, and visitors were welcome in each. "I rarely miss at least one of those," he said. Bec was the first indication to us that Christianity still had at least something of a presence in French culture.

From Bec we went on to Rouen, the capital city of Normandy, one of France's most historic cities and the site where Joan of Arc was burned at the stake in 1431. Poor Joan is not all that was burned: Rouen itself has been burned numerous times in the past 1000 years, most recently during the Allied invasion of Normandy in 1944. Since then it has been carefully rebuilt and, as we walked through the old section, we noticed it was virtually indistinguishable from how it likely would have been before the War.

Here at Rouen was a great example of the French conflict with religion. Joan of Arc is France's most notable religious heroine. She was canonized in 1920 and is the patron saint of France. A new church was built in her honor in Rouen in the 1970s and it was truly one of the most hideous, bizarre buildings I have ever seen. Spikes pointing into the sky are supposed to represent the flames that consumed this heroine, but who knows what the fish-shaped windows are supposed to mean. This monstrosity, it seemed to me, demonstrated nothing more than contempt for the Catholic Church and religion generally.

Not far from the shrine to Joan stands the Cathedral de Notre Dame, an eleventh century gothic cathedral, altered and added to at various times, but which maintains the splendor and dignity of pre-reformation cathedrals. I have visited dozens of European Gothic cathedrals; Rouen's certainly measures up to the best of them. But to the French, like the rest of the great religious monuments that appear in virtually every town, it is at best a museum. Mass is still celebrated on Sundays, and probably attracts a small group of celebrants, but otherwise tourists, mostly foreigners, traipse through the church, often sloppily dressed, with no appreciation for what this beautiful place represents. Nick and I had seen this all before, but could not help but wonder what the future held for Christianity in France.

From Rouen we rode on toward Caen, a city which felt the brunt of World War II more than about any other place in France: it was largely destroyed soon after the Normandy invasion, ultimately rebuilt as a modern industrial city, and stands in the midst of Allied cemeteries and battlefields. So much has been written about this that I will refrain from adding more here; there is little more to say other than the fact that the rows and rows of crosses, the monuments, and statues remain a moving experience, bringing vividly to mind the horror of war.

Ultimately we stopped, after another 100 km day, at the little village of Gavray, and found rooms in the most French of places—a shabby but clean little two-story hotel next to the railroad station, appropriately called Le Hotel de la Gare and the site of a little restaurant which provided a fabulous meal, washed down with a bottle of local red wine and ending with a calvados, an apple brandy native to Normandy. I couldn't help but comment to the owner, who was also the cook (and his wife, the waitress) that his French food was as good as it gets, but that after 100 km on a bicycle it tasted even better. He seemed very pleased.

The next day, Sunday, we proceeded through the fantastic and quite hilly Normandy countryside to Avranche. The Romanesque Cathedral there had been dismantled during the French Revolution and a revivalist Gothic Cathedral, Notre Dame de Champs, was built in the late nineteenth century as part of efforts to restore Catholicism to the region. But it and several other smaller Catholic churches were all closed and no masses offered, even though it was Sunday, demonstrating once again the extent to which France had abandoned any pretense that is was still a Christian country. Later in the day we did find two old and well-kept churches, but both were empty of people, no masses given. Just museums.

We then rode through fierce westerly winds along the Atlantic coast to Mont St. Michel, which in fact was visible from Avranche. One of the most visited places in France, it was crawling with tourists but a highly worthwhile stop. The Norman influence was very visible in the church, although there was some Gothic as well. We spent considerable time in the Abbey, which reminded us of the churches on Mt. Athos in the size and scope of the building, as well as its position in relation to the sea. Rather than being filled with the icons of the Orthodox Church, of course, it at least maintained the appearance of Catholic churches (if not the parishioners and celebrants) with medieval paintings, statues, and a Catholic altar. Once again, however, to the French people this great monument to Christianity was nothing more than a museum, as the tourist shops and little hotels perched up against the church indicated.

While there, we stopped at La Mère Poulard's, who reportedly makes "le plus célèbre omelette" in the world, and were not disappointed. Then, from Mont St. Michel we rode on to Rennes, about 70km away, which took the rest of the day. Rennes is the capital city of Brittany, known for its vibrant university and, for the tourists, its crooked medieval streets with half-timbered houses and Le Cathedral de St. Pierre, a large and imposing Gothic building. Much of the city was burned in the early eighteenth century, but parts of the old city remain, and the rest was well rebuilt.

We were trying to cover lots of ground on this trip, so it was back onto the bikes and onward through Guerche to St. Denis d'Anjou (117 km later). Here we found a small auberge that happened to have a couple of rooms, and proved to be one of the highlights of the trip—more from a tourist than a pilgrim's perspective, but one of those memorable evenings that live in memory for many years. The place was run by a rather overweight fellow with a droopy mustache and tousled hair and his dapper, trim, and well-dressed wife. After we got settled our host inquired what we would like to eat, gave a couple of suggestions, and then went off to the market to get the fresh lamb and a few other things. Of course, the meal was fantastic, particularly good after so many miles, paired with a fine local red wine and polished off with calvados.

After a sumptuous breakfast in the garden the next morning, we went on our way toward the Abby of St. Pierre at Solemne, one of the great monasteries in France. We had hoped to be able to stay there for a couple of days, reigniting our faith in the beautiful old site still full of monks, and in fact had been led to believe from the guidebooks that a stay would be possible. But the monk at the front gate was most discouraging, telling us he was sorry but such a visit was not possible. But when he realized I was an American, he summoned the one resident American monk. Bounding down the stairs appeared a fellow with red hair and a beard, introducing himself as Michael Bozell. When I introduced myself Michael broke out laughing, said that of course we could stay for as long as we liked, and showed us to our rooms.

Our visit to Solemne, facilitated by what appeared to be a

coincidence, would prove to be the most valuable time on the trip. Michael showed us through the monastery and, before any discussion about what we should expect, suggested that we spend some time in the church before supper. Vespers would begin in a while, just before the meal, he said, but we should take some time beforehand to be quiet. Here was as peaceful a place as one could imagine; there were monks and a few others deep in prayer. As I sat there thinking about my life, this trip, where we were, and thanking God for my good fortune, I had the feeling that somebody else was sitting beside me—a sense that I had never had before or since. This would truly be a place where my faith would be reinforced.

Founded in about 1000 AD, Solemnes was one of the oldest Benedictine monasteries in the world. Like every other religious institution in France, it was shut down during the French Revolution, and had been shuttered four more times by the French government since, but bounced back each time. Michael, a most forthcoming host, explained its long and con-voluted history. The Abbey was shaped something like a shoe, he explained. The Sentlé River was on one side and the village and a convent on the other. It was home to some seventy-five monks, he told us, and one of the two largest monasteries in France. If there is a flame of Christianity still burning in France, it burns brightly at the abbey of Solemnes.

Solemnes is renowned as the intellectual home and primary research facility in the world for the renaissance of the Gregorian chant. This was part of the contribution to Catholicism ema-nating from the Abbey, Michael explained. The priest who rees-tablished the abbey after the French Revolution, Michael told us, did so to bring to life the "pure traditions" of Catholicism, namely the centrality of the Vatican and the Pope. He later contributed to the formation of the doctrines of infallibility and the Immaculate Conception, and finally to the Gregorian chant.

Abbey at Solemnes, France

I had known that there was a Bozell monk somewhere in France, but had no idea where. What good fortune and what a surprise it was to run into him at Solemne! Michael Bozell was, for me, the perfect host. He was close in age to being my contemporary, his brother Brent remains a close friend and his mother, Trish, worked for me as an editor for many years, was also a close friend, and edited the one major book that I wrote as her last project. Michael grew up in an environment somewhat similar to mine and in a family that my family had known well since the 1950s. My father had published *God and Man at Yale*, the book that launched William F. Buckley, Jr., Michael's uncle, in 1951; a few years later my father published a book on Joe McCarthy by Buckley and Michael's father, and had remained friends with both for the rest of their lives. So finally meeting—and being able to have a leisurely conversation with—this contemporary who had become a Benedictine monk in France was indeed a once-in-a-lifetime experience.

"So, how did you ever wind up here, as a monk?" I asked him. He told me that he had been adrift after college, had a few odd jobs but with no apparent goal. The son of a famous father and nephew of a more famous one, he was one of ten children and had been brought up in a very Catholic household. In order to be on his own and find his way, he travelled through Europe in the 1970s, and stopped at Solemnes, where he stayed as a guest for several weeks. He left and came back several times, and finally was granted permission to become a novice at the abbey where he would be assessed to determine whether or not he met the standards necessary to become a full-fledged member of the Benedictine Order.

He had not only succeeded, but had become a vibrant member of the monastery, taking on a variety of duties, and seven years before our visit was ordained a priest. At his ordination, some fifty members of the Buckley-Bozell family congregated at Solemnes for his ordination—beautifully recounted in Buckley's autobiography of faith, *Nearer My God*—an event which was probably virtually unique in the history of French monasticism. Michael had become fluent in French and proficient in Latin, he told me—the two languages used at the abbey—and spent much of his time, while not in prayer, doing translations and research.

Nick asked Michael why monks feel the need to be removed from the rest of the world, to spend their days, and in fact the rest of their lives, in prayer and silence.

"Our vows," Michael responded, "are poverty, chastity and obedience. When we are admitted, as full-fledged monks, our obligation is for the rest of our lives. But that also means it is into the next life as well." He went on to explain that the worldly separation was largely to free a monk from the desire for possessions and attachments which might separate them from their duty of solitude and the "quest for God"—the heart of the Benedictine order.

After Michael was ordained as a priest, his uncle William F. Buckley, Jr. asked whether, "the temptations of a secular nature will always be there: seductive, to be resisted at the cost of great spiritual agony?" Michael responded that indeed there was a daily conflict, among all members of the order, "between the natural pining of our appetites" and the spiritual imperative to transcend everything else. The men who become monks, he went on, are radicals by temperament. There are other ways to be a Christian, but, he told Buckley, "The monk's life is a continuous striving, a daily battle, and the prize, the summit of the mountain, is Christ."

The dedication of these men to God—their faith—was palpable. In a country that has all but obliterated Christianity, the faith lives on in the hearts and souls of these men in this starkly beautiful and uncomplicated place. What a joy it was to spend a couple of days here, days in silence and in prayer, with time to reflect on my existence and situation. The greater impact of the experience probably came over the ensuing years, as I thought back on those days I spent observing and listening to these pious men in their contemplative life.

Afterwards we rode along the Loire, stopping at a couple of the famous Chateaux, went on to Tours and ultimately, jumping ahead on a train, to Orléans. The next morning, across vast fields of grain and against strong headwinds, we biked to Chartres, the site of one of Europe's most famous cathedrals. As with the others, it was full of tourists admiring the architecture and stonework but seemingly oblivious to the fact that it was a church. But such is France.

We thought of riding on into Paris, but were warned by the proprietor of the restaurant where we had lunch that traffic would likely consume us, so we took a train to the Paris Montparnasse Station. We then did brave the rush-hour traffic, riding across the city to the Gare du Nord, where Nick boarded the Chunnel train to London.

The next couple of days by myself in Paris gave me plenty of time to reflect on the trip and what we had experienced. I pedaled from one end of the city to the other, spent several hours in the Louvre, found a wonderful concert of French baroque music, fell into conversation with a variety of people, and just soaked in the best of France.

France, the country once virtually synonymous with Catholicism—home to some 45,000 Catholic churches in every town and village, with public holidays that are almost all Christian in origin, and the home of countless saints like Joan of Arc and countless Catholic writers and intellectuals—had become virtually agnostic. Some French Christians argue that France may not be as dead as some like to believe. A majority of the population is composed of "cultural Catholics"—they went to Catholic schools and get married and baptize their children in Catholic churches, even if they make no other efforts to practice the faith. The names of their towns, villages, and streets often related, in one way or another, to the Catholic Church. So the places such as the Abbeys at Bec and Solemnes maintain the intellectual firepower and adherence to the Catholic order that may, over time, reignite the flame that once was so prevalent.

Besides the wonderful sights, food and wine, great conversations and plenty of exercise, our cycling pilgrimage provided a short but penetrating glimpse into France and its culture, and a chance to observe and reflect on the state of Christian faith in France and what it meant.

As I spent that beautiful spring day in Paris, I could not help but be reminded constantly of Jonathan Aitken. His perjury conviction had its origins, several years earlier, at the Ritz Hotel in Paris, and culminated when he lied, while under oath, that he had not stayed there. Needless to say, his accommodations at the Ritz were certainly a far cry from what he was experiencing on that June day somewhere in a prison in England. What I know about him now, having found his faith and lived his life ever since as a faithful Christian, I wonder if France, now in the depths of secularism, may also find its way and return to being a Christian country.

But for me, I thought that if rural France has largely abandoned Christianity and Paris become an agnostic playground, how could one criticize a couple of days, without obligation or duties, in Paris in June?

4

NICAEA, THE SEVEN CHURCHES OF REVELATION AND CAPPADOCIA, TURKEY

June, 2000

AFTER VISITING THE MONASTERIES on Mt. Athos, walking the Camino, and bicycling across Normandy—all places where Christianity had flourished during the Middle Ages—Nick suggested that it might be worthwhile to explore some of the places that are actually mentioned in the Bible, and particularly where the early church had developed. He suggested a trip to Turkey to visit the Seven Churches of Revelation. These were all, he explained, major Roman outposts in what was then known as simply Asia where there had been a Christian presence, that John had written letters of encouragement and advice to them which were included in the very early parts of the Book of Revelation.

I was beginning to realize, even after the first three trips, just how broad a phenomenon Christianity actually was, what a huge impact it has had historically, politically, and philosophically, and agreed that looking at what had been going on a millennium earlier than the eleventh and twelfth centuries might be interesting. I had also read a good deal about the Nicene Creed and had become interested in how it had come about and how it had settled one of the great disputes of all time. So a side trip to Nicaea would make sense. Besides, Turkey was an interesting place politically in the year 2000, and provided an almost endless list of places to visit.

I met Nick in Istanbul at the hotel bar late on a warm June evening to embark on another pilgrimage together, this time to see Nicaea and the seven churches.

After a couple days in Istanbul, we rented a car, took a ferry across the Sea of Marmara, and drove to Iznik, the Turkish city which incorporates the ancient city of Nicaea. Where the earlier trips provided plenty of exercise—a big part of what every pilgrimage should be—this one would have to be a road trip, as the distances were just too vast. Nicea was the site of the third Christian council of 325 AD where the Nicene Creed, recited by every Christian during virtually every mass or service, was negotiated and written, and sent out to the Christian world as the foundation of Christian belief. This creed, called by the Emperor Constantine in response to the Arian heresy that was tearing the Roman Empire apart, established as doctrine that God and Jesus Christ were operating on the same plane, were equals, and in fact that Jesus was God. Most of the 200 or so bishops of the church met at Constantine's summer palace for several weeks and hammered out the creed which was to stand as the final authority on just who Jesus Christ was.

The actual site of the Council is now under water, but walls still surround much of the ancient city, and there still exist many foundations and other ruins built by the Romans and during the Ottoman period. Nick and I found a comfortable spot on one of the walls and he explained to me what was at stake when the Creed was negotiated. We then read through the Creed, stopping at the end of each clause to discuss what it meant. "Notice," Nick told me, "that there are only four lines about God, and four lines about the Holy Spirit. But Christ gets fully twenty lines."

I had never thought of it that way. "An interesting way to recognize what they were trying to do with the Creed," I responded. Afterall, the Creed's purpose was to establish Christ as equal to God, so that much explanation was needed to make it clear to the Aryans that God and Jesus Christ were equal partners. Sitting on the ruins of an ancient Roman wall on that summer evening, the sun going down over the hills on the western horizon, imagining what went on 1700 years ago, and read about how it came to be and why, is a scene which comes to mind every time I recite the Creed.

The next day we headed to the first of the cities of the seven churches mentioned in the book of Revelation. About the only easily comprehensible part of Revelation, found near the beginning, is a series of letters written to the seven churches of Asia. The apostle John the Evangelist wrote Revelation near the end of his life, between 70 and 90 AD. At the time, there were several Christian churches established in Roman cities in Asia Minor—now Turkey—cities of no small consequence to Rome, mostly with populations of 50,000 or more and controlling a rich trading and resource region of the empire. They were built, as most Roman cities were at the time, with great temples, coliseums, theaters and the rest, mostly on the eastern Aegean coast, accessible to Rome by ship.

John probably visited most of the seven cities and their churches, and was well aware of their circumstances, their strengths and weaknesses, and their relationship with the Romans. In fact, John spent much of his later life in Ephesus, died there, and was buried at what later became the site of St. John's Cathedral.

In suggesting that we visit the seven churches, Nick thought they, and the other places he had suggested in Turkey, would be a wonderful way to learn about the many trials that early Christians had, and how the Church fathers dealt with them. John's letters, he told me, are readily understandable, historic yet timely, and full of understanding of the human spirit and man's faith. They would provide a profound lesson about our everyday dealings with life and faith.

The Revelation letters remind one of the ruthless power of the Roman Empire in those days, how it dominated the world. And in light of that strength, they further remind of what a powerless group these Christians were, how totally vulnerable and virtually powerless yet fanatical they must have seemed to the proud Romans. But John's letters display the incredible power that the Christian faith had, and just how concerned the Romans were about the Christian message and the extent to which it threatened them. It was a tremendous lesson for me in the power of belief and of faith to see the ruins of those magnificent cities and their coliseums, marble streets, baths, and theaters, to feel the sheer sense of how Roman dominance and power was set against the apparently hopeless little band of Christians, religious fanatics without power or money. For it was the Christians, of course, who ultimately prevailed and those great Roman cities which are now in ruins.

Each of the Asian cities had a small group of Christians—always a minority, always persecuted, always under pressure from the Romans to worship Caesar instead of Christ. Some biblical scholars believe that John's letters to the seven churches of Asia were literally dictated to John by Jesus at the end of his life. John says, at the end of Chapter One of Revelation, that Christ told him to write these letters: "Write the things which thou hast seen and the things which are, and the things which shall be hereafter."

To each of the churches John writes words of praise, and to all but two words of criticism. Each letter reflects some specific trait of the city where the church was (by "church" John does not mean a church as we think of one today, but rather a group of Christians living and worshipping together in their Roman cities). The criticisms John writes are much more, however, than just criticisms of those churches, but are commentaries on common human failings or attributes—as topical today as they were in the first century.

Pergamum, known in ancient times as Pergamos, was the first of the seven churches on our venture. Pergamum was one of the capitals of the Roman province of Asia, and the greatest city in Asia Minor according to the Roman writer Pliny. It was a literary center, with a library of some 200,000 books, and also a center of religious teaching and worship of the pagan gods; to John it was Satan's seat, a center of Caesar worship. Some of the Christians there—and it was probably a relatively small group—had been tempted by these pagans and had engaged in false teaching and lured toward the sins of idolatry and immorality. So in his letter, John at first praises them, but then admonishes them for their sins and warns them that if they do not repent, the Lord will punish them—that he will wage war against his own people. These few Christians addressed by John were always far overshadowed by the pagans, who made their life, in a word, miserable. According to the English writer William Barclay in his *Letters to the Seven Churches*, "In Pergamum the Christians, in all their weakness and their helplessness, had to preserve their loyalty against the imperial might of Caesar worship. But even in Pergamum men held fast to the name of Jesus Christ and refused to deny their faith in him."

Pergamum sits high on a hill with incredible views of the surrounding plains. We walked through the ruins of the basilica, the church John had written to (later a mosque), and various rebuilt Roman structures—much more than we would find at the other seven churches, with the exception of Ephesus. Ruins and recreations though they were, they were enough to give an idea of the importance of the place in biblical times, at least from the standpoint of Rome.

As the first of these places we would visit, Pergamum was a lesson in the power of the Roman Empire opposed the challenges that the Christians experienced, not the least of which was, as John told them, their worship of pagan gods. This lesson would be repeated six more times, in the other six churches, and again later in Cappadoccia. It is probably safe to say that not one of these sites was definitive in that lesson, but by the end of the trip, it was overwhelming.

But for Christians, according to St. John, it was Satan's

throne. Yet despite the problems there, they held onto Jesus's name, as loyal Christians always should do.

From Pergamum we drove on to Thyatira, second on our itinerary. It was the least important of the seven cities, but was the church that received the longest letter. Most of the ancient structures of Thyatira had been destroyed 1500 years ago; it was now a modern commercial city with the remains of a church surrounded by grass and trees in the center of the town. There was not much to see, but we found a comfortable place to sit and read the letter to the church. John begins by praising the Christians for their "love and faith, service and perseverance," of the church there. But there is a woman known as "Jezebel," who is apparently a prophetess who is tempting the people into immorality. Nevertheless, John said, both the faithful and the unfaithful would be repaid according to their deeds.

"Not much has changed in 2000 years," I reflected to Nick. He agreed that the Jezebels of the world are still very much alive, and her men, when they stop to consider it, very worried about what might lie in store.

The next stop was Sardis. We faced a long and tedious drive along a highway teeming with big trucks, motorcycles, and tractors chugging along at a snail's pace, plenty of pollution—very much an early twenty-first-century experience one could find in almost any corner of the world.

Sardis had two temples, one only a mile or so from the other. The first was on a well-preserved Roman road, still paved and good enough to drive along. It was an imposing place, partially restored, and included a nearby bath, a latrine (a stone toilet seat, capable of seating eight people in a row, with a small aqueduct underneath to carry away the waste, was still virtually usable—although I did not try it out). Besides the temple itself, there were a sports arena and several other buildings first built between 200 and 500 BC and rebuilt many times over many years. A mile or so away stood the other temple, part of the same establishment, and just as large and imposing as the first, back from the road, surrounded by hills and trees. Inside the temple stood a small church—literally built in a corner inside what had been a great Roman temple—the church dating to about 700 AD and which had remained a Christian church into the beginning of the Ottoman Empire. Now it was simply part of the ruins. Nick mentioned that it looked as though the church, built inside this great Roman temple and one tenth its size, was a sort of rebuke to the Romans—"your great empire may have built vast complexes, but our church survives."

Sardis was a large and important trading center and the junction of several important roads. Wealth poured in, but so did decadence: Barclay says its people "were notoriously loose-living, notoriously pleasure-and luxury-loving." The wealthier it became—and it became very wealthy—the more it lost all claim to greatness. Life had become decadent. And so had the Christian church. According to John's letter, the church at Sardis was at peace—but it was the peace of the dead. It was not threatened by any of the forces threatening the other six churches—not Caesar worship or persecution, no malignant slanders, not even threats from within. Materially it was alive; spiritually it was dead. As John wrote,

> I know your deeds; you have a reputation of being alive, but you are dead. Wake up! Strengthen what remains and is about to die, for I have found your deeds unfinished in

the sight of my God. Remember, therefore, what you have received and heard; hold it fast, and repent. But if you do not wake up, I will come like a thief, and you will not know at what time I will come to you.

We sat on a bench at the side of the Roman road and talked about what all of this meant. The first lesson in John's letter, Nick remarked, is that Christ, like a thief, will appear when we least expect him to; he is ever vigilant of our sins and if Christians do not live a life of daily relationship with him and exercise daily repentance, we will not only be subject to his threat, but never know when to expect punishment.

I asked Nick if what this was all about was not rather poignant for today's Western Christian churches. The problems facing Christianity, I thought, were nothing new but had been alive and well in ancient Sardis. America was secure and Europe even more so. Communism had been defeated and there was no enemy staring Europe or the U.S. in the face; life was easy, wealth unprecedented. People had every material thing they had ever dreamed of having, and more. As wealth increased on both sides of the Atlantic, greatness had dissipated. The culture, like ancient Sardis, had become decadent. Many Europeans and Americans were "notoriously loose-living, notoriously pleasure- and luxury-loving." Even the Church was too often concerned more with process than substance, with ritual than purpose, with material than spiritual things. Like the church at Sardis, much of modern Christian culture was effectively dead.

I'm not sure that Nick agreed with that harsh assessment.

It was not far to Philadelphia which, in ancient times, lay on the principal road from Europe to Asia; the city was literally the gateway from one continent to another. It was a missionary city, spreading Greek culture, language, way of life into the wild world of the barbarous tribes of Asia. Later, in early Christian times, Philadelphia was destined to spread Christianity, and all it represented, in those same wild and untamed lands. Philadelphia was the open door of opportunity to the virgin territory of the East.

As we walked up from the parking area, the harsh and barren-looking landscape stretched for miles to the East. An elderly man, whose English was tortured but understandable, approached us and offered to show us around for a few coins. He had grown up nearby and seemed well-versed in the history and geography of the place. Because of the volcanic activity, he told us, soil in the region was fertile and crops had once grown well. He said the region had previously been known for its fruits, vegetables, and even fine wines—even, he told us, as was described in the Bible, but because of the instability of the geology, frequent volcanic eruptions and earthquakes, agriculture had long since disappeared.

Unlike Sardis, according to John's letter, Philadelphia remained a faithful city of the Church. Accordingly, Jesus Christ in Revelation rewarded Philadelphia with peace and saved it from devastation by its enemies: "Because you have kept my command to persevere, I also will keep you from the hour of trial which shall come upon the whole world, to test those who dwell on the earth." To this day Philadelphia remains a Christian city, with Christian values, and a Christian faith.

Laodicea lay not far away, spanning a huge open area on the top of a hill. As Nick and I approached it, we saw huge ruins of temples dominating the hilltop, some reconstructed, but others just as they had deteriorated over 2,000 years. Because of the warm and dry climate in this part of the world, Nick mentioned, these ancient structures survived better than in cold and wet Northern Europe. There were two theaters, each large enough to seat a couple of thousand people. Laodicea was an important part of the Roman Empire, situated at the confluence of two rivers. It was the location of a Roman judicial court, a trading center, and very wealthy, the hub of banking for the vicinity. The earthquakes that laid waste to Sardis and Philadelphia also devastated Laodicea, but each time it was rebuilt, grander than before, with its own wealth. The Laodicean's considered themselves self-sufficient—they had so much money that they could manage without help from others, or from God. So the Laodiceans put their faith not in God, but in material wealth, in luxury, and in fitness and health. Their culture was built on high living and material benefits provided to all the people. It was, in fact, an ancient welfare state. For this, they earned a stern rebuke in Revelation:

> I know your deeds, that you are neither cold nor hot. I wish you were either one or the other! So, because you are luke-warm—neither hot nor cold—I am about to spit you out of my mouth. You say, "I am rich; I have acquired wealth and do not need a thing." But you do not realize that you are wretched, pitiful, poor, blind and naked…. Those that I love I rebuke and discipline. So be earnest and repent.

Laodicea, and the lessons that it drew in Revelation, seemed to me to provide the most poignant lesson to current Western civilization. It spoke of many of the same things that were hot topics in Washington and the rest of the US, as well as in Europe. Particularly among American conservatives—the vast materialism and wealth enjoyed by our culture, the luxury, and even the great emphasis on fitness and health seemed to parallel the situation in Laodicea. The Laodicean culture, as that of the United States and Western Europe, was built on high living and material benefits, increasingly made available to much of the population. Faith, as it had become in Laodicea, had largely been abandoned in Europe and was suffering a similar decline across North and South America. To say faith was "lukewarm" in much of the world would, as a result, not be much of an exaggeration.

Our next stop, Aphrodesias, was not one of the Seven. We debated whether it was worth the drive—it was off the beaten path, far back into the hills on a poor road. But from the description in the guidebooks, I commented to Nick that had it been one of the Seven Churches, John no doubt would have had rather harsh words to say. The City was built to honor Aphrodite, the goddess of sex and love. It was what scholars describe as an open-air bordello.

Aside from the fact that it was not part of our Biblical venture, Aphrodesias was perhaps the best example that we saw of what a large Roman city must have looked like—much of the ancient structures remained almost as if they had been recently built, and others had been well restored. New York University initiated an excavation project in the 1960s, and built a modern museum displaying marble statues, pillars, and many other artifacts found on the site. What is left of Aphrodesias is considered one of the most important Greco-Roman cities in the Mideast. A small theater, still in good repair, stood next to a much larger theater which must have seated 10,000 people or more. As with many of these theaters, the acoustics were perfect: Nick stood on what had been the stage, I went to the last row, probably at least 50 yards from him, and could hear every word he spoke as if he were right next to me. A stadium with seating for 30,000, with a track at least a kilometer long with a bit of cleaning and removing debris, could have hosted an NFL football game. According to the guide who showed us around, the stone carvings, sculptures, and remains of buildings are among the best Greek ruins in the world.

The crown jewel of our pilgrimage was Ephesus, the most famous and the grandest of the seven churches. Situated at the mouth of a river and the crossing of three important trade routes, Ephesus was the *Vanity Fair* of the Ancient World; its commerce made it one of the wealthiest cities of its time and extremely politically important. It had been granted status as a free city by the Romans, meaning that it was self-governing. An "assize" town, it was a place where Roman justice was dispensed by the visiting governor, all in full Roman grandeur, and with a population of a quarter of a million people. Ephesus was also a religious center and the site of one of the great temples of that part of the world—the temple of Diana, nearly as big as St. Peter's Basilica in Rome. Pagan worship during Roman times was an orgy. Amidst shouting, music, and burning of incense, worshipers would work themselves into an emotional frenzy where participants would wallow in sexual excess. Morally, ancient Ephesus was a vile and nasty place, full of cruel people with morals worse than beasts. (As one wag said, at least dogs and beasts don't mutilate each other while fornicating.) Yet Paul stayed in Ephesus for over three years. According to Barclay, "it is said that it is hard to be a Christian in a modern, industrial, competitive civilization. Let us remember Ephesus, and let us remember that there were Christians there."

After our arrival in Ephesus, we walked to the ruins of St. John's church—where John the Evangelist is buried—found a comfortable place to sit, and read John's letter to the church at Ephesus. The church there, wrote John, had plenty of energy, where hard work and perseverance on behalf of Christ was ubiquitous. It was also a church where true Christianity—call it Christian orthodoxy—was well preserved. The church could not stand wicked people (and there were plenty of them in Ephesus). But John writes that Ephesus lacked the most important Christian attribute—Christian love. The lack of love overcame all the good that energy and orthodoxy provided: "I have somewhat against thee, because thou hast left thy first love."

Ephesus is the best preserved of the seven, and is said to be the best place in the world to get a sense of what life in Roman times was like. We walked through the city, with temples, theaters, columns, the remains of houses, even sheds well preserved. We walked through the ruins of the Library of Celsus, considered one of the most beautiful buildings in the Roman Empire which contained some 12,000 scrolls. Our hired guide, a friendly and well-spoken fellow probably in his sixties, took us through again, explaining each nook and cranny in detail. Although he had undoubtedly done it a thousand times, he took delight in explaining it all, recounting what life must have been like in ancient times. We stopped at the little theater where Paul would hold forth each day, talking with the crowd that surrounded him, preaching the Gospel, praying, trying to convert people to Christianity—until, that is, he got into a terrible row with the local jewelry craftsmen and had to pack up and leave in a hurry.

The Library, Ephesus, Turkey

⚞ Our guide told us that local legend claims that John lived in Ephesus for a time, although John makes no such claim in his letter to the Ephesian Church. He is generally praiseworthy of the Ephesian Christians, who he describes as hardworking, devoted to search for the truth, and holding to the central truth about God with courage and perseverance. His only criticism is that they have left behind their "first love," that the love of God had become theoretical. As we talked about this, sitting on a wall overlooking the city, Nick explained that scholars puzzled over just what John meant. John's letter seemed clear enough that they were thorough in their resistance to idolatry, but not sufficiently devoted to the alternative, or God and Jesus Christ.

A few kilometers from Ephesus, on top of Bulbul Mountain, we found the house where the Virgin Mary, brought there by John, is believed to have spent her last days and is buried. A holy place indeed. It is preserved as a Christian site—one of the very few in Turkey.

Finally: Smyrna—modern day Izmir, one of the largest cities in modern Turkey. Even in ancient times it was large, rich, and important. During the second century it was the center for Caesar worship, which was devised by the Romans as a way of holding the empire together. Each Roman citizen, once a year, was required to burn a pinch of incense and recite that Caesar was lord, was given a certificate, and could then worship as he pleased.

Most interesting to us was the Church of St. Polycarp, a beautiful, small and peaceful Catholic church, built in the eleventh century in the midst of a noisy and bustling part of the city—one of those places where, upon entering, I felt an immense serenity and quiet. This holy site was enveloped in the peace of Christ. Like Mary's home near Ephesus, the Turkish government allows this church to stay open and to celebrate Mass for the Catholics who live in Izmir.

I had heard of Polycarp, but knew little about him, so when I returned home I read about him and subsequently have given several talks in and around Washington about him. He was the bishop of Smyrna, one of the most noted and famous Christians of his time, beloved by the people of Smyrna but a constant thorn in the side of the Romans. One feast day, when he was eighty-six, Polycarp was seized by Jews—who heavily populated Smyrna—and taken to the stadium, full of a loud and boisterous crowd. Worship Caesar, Polycarp was told, or be burned at the stake. He gave his immortal answer:

> Eighty and six years have I served Christ, and He has done me no ill. How can I blaspheme my King who hath served me? I fear not the fire that burns for a season and after a while is quenched. Why do you delay? Come, do your will.

So they tied him to the stake, and lit the fire. As the flames licked his body, he prayed his great prayer:

> Today I thank Thee for allowing me to share the cup of Christ and the martyrs through which the body and soul will be resurrected in the eternity of the spirit. And I ask Thee to accept me as a worthy sacrifice of incense in the place of those standing before Thee.

Polycarp, it seemed to me, exemplified the courage and conviction of many of the early Christians, men and women who were willing to die for their beliefs. As I gave my talks on Polycarp, the questions would usually turn to whether anybody in today's world would be so brave. Probably not many, was the usual response.

In the letter to Smyrna in Revelation, John warned of oncoming persecution but wrote: "Do not be afraid of what you are about to suffer. I tell you, the devil will put some of you in prison to test you, and you will suffer persecution for ten days. Be faithful, even to the point of death, and I will give your life as your victor's crown."

We travelled on to Cappadocia, south of Ankara, once part of the Persian Empire, later Greek and later Roman. It became an important Christian site in the third and fourth centuries and is particularly famous for its underground cities, where Christians would hide from Roman persecutors.

We drove along the Marmara Sea to the Dardanelles, past Gallipoli, scene of one of the great battles of World War I—a battle where over 100,000 soldiers died and which was the birthplace of democratic Turkey led by Ataturk. From there we went on to Troy, the buried city discovered and excavated by the German businessman-archeologist Heinrich Schliemann in the 1870s, situated on the Aegean and at the entry to the Hellespont. From there, down a winding road to the sea, we arrived at the little town of Assos, across the bay from the Island of Lesbos. Paul visited Assos twice, once sailing from Troy and once on foot, on a return trip from Alexandria in Greece to meet St. Luke who, according to Acts, had come to Assos as well. With the exception of a few cars parked on the quay it probably didn't look much different than it did in 53 AD when Paul arrived. As I walked down the beach I could almost visualize Paul coming toward me.

The modern part of Assos is on a high bank overlooking the sea; down a windy and narrow road we came to a small cluster of stone houses wedged between the steep cliff and the beach. Our hotel was right on the water with a couple of tables outside overlooking the Aegean; as we ate our supper of fresh fish and a wonderful green salad, Lesbos in the background, it was again easy to imagine the Apostle Paul striding up the beach. We talked for hours about this place, its appearance in the Book of

Acts, about Paul and what he must have been like.

The trip to the Seven Churches was the first outside of Europe and into the Middle East. Turkey, in the year 2000 was still a peaceful and pro-Western country and although Islam was virtually ubiquitous, Westerners and non-Christians were welcomed and respected. So from the standpoint of geopolitics, the culture and the many historical sites we visited it was enlightening.

As a journey to one of the historical treasures of Christendom, the trip could not have been a better introduction to the history of the early church. To visit places which are not only in the Bible, but which play a significant part, sheds new light into the eyes of a new Christian, at least it did into mine. To sit on a wall built by Romans, overlooking the site where the Nicene Creed was actually negotiated and written; to visit a little stone village on the shores of the Aegean Sea where Paul walked, not once but twice; to visit the ruins of a city where Paul preached (and was chased out of town); all of these seared a memory into my head that will never leave, and made the lessons we learn as Christians alive in a way that they could otherwise never be.

5

SYRIA

June 2001

SOMETIME EARLY IN 2001 Nick and I started talking about
another trip. The others had worked out well not only as journeys, but also as pilgrimages. They were enormously instructive
to me for my faith and interest in the history of Christianity, not
to mention historically, culturally and geopolitically. During the
previous trip to Turkey, we had seen some of the great cities of
the Roman Empire where Christians had lived and contributed
to the development of the early church, but which had been
virtually shuttered first by the Ottomans and more recently by
modern Turkish Islam. Nick suggested going further into the
Muslim world; he had been to the Holy Land already, so suggested places such as Jordan, Lebanon, or perhaps Syria.

Here was a place that had many Biblical reference points, not
the least of which was Paul's conversion on the road to Damascus;
there were also many ruins and other interesting ancient Christian

sites, including some of the oldest Christian churches in the world. And although largely a Muslim country, Syrian Muslims had a reputation of being relatively easy-going, did not persecute Christians, and in fact, in 2001, nearly a quarter of all Syrians were Christians. This was, remember, early in 2001, months before the 9/11 attack on the World Trade Center and the Pentagon. Syria was still off the beaten path, at least for American tourists, rarely was mentioned in the papers, and was not much of a factor in international affairs. Also, prior to 9/11, Islam was still an afterthought in most Westerners' minds, and Christians, at least in the U.S. and Europe, rarely thought about it. Nick mentioned that although there was plenty to see there, Syria was not considered much of a pilgrimage destination—something that made it all the more interesting to us.

I read what I could find before the trip, including Robert Kaplan's *Eastward to Tartary*, a rollicking good story about the author's trek from Budapest to Turkmenistan, with a side trip through Syria and Jordan to Israel. Kaplan has a wonderful way of combining politics, culture, scenery and people into a lively and compelling narrative, and his description of Syria was sufficiently vivid that it made me want to go there. In addition, Nick and I agreed that I would seek out several Syrians or Syrian experts in Washington before leaving, and Nick would do the same, in London, with religious and historical experts. By the time we were ready to leave, we agreed that we felt well-supplied with lists of people to meet, places to visit, and sites to see, and that we could combine the pilgrimage with an interesting look at Middle Eastern history and current-day politics.

Little did we know, of course, what would transpire in this little corner of the world over the next couple of decades. As you, dear reader, will learn, we were privileged to be among the last generation of pilgrims to have visited some of the oldest sites in the Christian world—places such as a Street called Straight in Damascus, where the Apostle Paul was let down from the city wall in a basket, and villages where Aramaic, Jesus Christ's language, was still spoken. Many of these were later blown up by Islamic radicals and by the bombs tossed around by the Syrian government, the Russians, and our own U.S. Air Force.

Arriving in Damascus in 2001 was something like arriving in Phnom Penh, Bucharest, Thessalonica or any number of other third world cities. The place was shabby and run down, the airport old but reasonably clean; security was lackadaisical; a few beggars, scrawny dogs, and dirty children milled around, and plenty of tiny little four-door cabs waited for a fare into the city. The deal at the Sultan Hotel included airport pick-up, and as I walked through the line at security there was a skinny little Arab fellow holding up a sign with my name. He whisked me through the lines that had formed for cabs and moneychangers and off we went to the Sultan. It was not as grand as the name implied.

Hafez al-Assad, the Syrian president—read: dictator—had died a little more than a year before, and Syria appeared to be losing a little of its Warsaw Pact–like mentality and appearance. Much of the repression, if not gone, had loosened up. Travel was unrestricted and Syria was considered a reasonably safe place to visit. Assad's younger son, Bashar, had just come to power a year before my arrival, and was busily trying to make people aware of the fact that he was in charge: Billboards and posters were everywhere—large ones, small ones, postcards, and everything in between—extolling his virtue as a leader and reminding the Syrians that he was in charge. He was a rather twerpy looking fellow, appeared to be about eighteen (he was thirty-six at the time) with a scraggly mustache cultivated, it was quite obvious, to add a few years to his youthful visage.

Young Assad was practicing ophthalmology in London when his Stalinist father died. Married to an elegant and leggy London socialite from a well-to-do Syrian family who worked at Morgan Stanley, he had been called back to Damascus upon his father's death to fill in for his older brother Bassel, the heir apparent who had wrapped his Mercedes around a tree at 180 kilometers an hour in 1994. Poor Bashar appeared lost in his new role, and left control to the bagmen and thugs who had run things for his father.

But one thing struck me above all else, and was not lost on most who saw his picture: he looked scared. Given what would happen to his country over the next dozen or so years, it is no wonder that he did.

Assad appeared to be neither loved nor hated. Although the cult of personality was his goal, and the marketing tool was thousands and thousands of photos of himself, most people seemed unconcerned about him and his government, and as a tourist I certainly did not get the impression that the government was particularly oppressive. Standing up on a soapbox on a busy street and denouncing the young up-and-coming dictator would be ill-advised, and it was said that there were several thousand political prisoners locked up in prisons scattered around the Syrian desert, but the place seemed a great deal freer than anything I ever observed behind the Iron Curtain during the old Soviet Union days. In fact, a rather common exchange with a Syrian, when it became apparent that I was an American, went something like this: "So, you are an American. I don't care for your government much, but then I don't like our government much either. I cannot do anything about my government—it is what it is—and I assume you cannot do anything about yours either. But let's be friends."

Damascus was a teeming place with cars everywhere, going every which way as fast as they could travel. The narrow streets were full of people and abounded with restaurants and street merchants, and the souks (markets), which seemed to go on for miles through tunnels and basements, building to building, were full of clothes, jewelry, copper ware, electronics, and much else. People were mostly neat and clean, but clothes were often old and shabby though well pressed. Many of the women were dressed in quasi-Muslim garb, but many Syrians were in western clothing, and most were friendly and helpful.

Can I show you anything, they would ask, or take you somewhere? Whenever we were sitting in a café, a conversation would invariably start up with other customers and almost instant friends were made. People in the shops, the cab drivers, guides, and docents in public places all seemed to want to help these itinerant westerners.

I walked for miles through Damascus—into the old city and the souk, up and down Straight Street (and knew I would come back to this Christian site once Nick arrived) into back streets, mosques, and Christian churches. The city gave a mixed impression, with Soviet-style apartment buildings next to a street that might be 1500 years old. In the souk I was approached by a polite and well-dressed fellow who spoke English well. After a few minutes he asked if he could buy me a coffee, and we fell into a long conversation. He was more interested in Syria's rich cultural history than politics. Syrians, he told me, were an enormously creative people who relished their past and were enormously proud of what their ancestors had built. Visit our museums, our old buildings, the Roman and Greek antiquities, he urged me. We would find them well-preserved and manned by willing guides to show us around. Above all, he said, Syrians wanted a peaceful life, surrounded by friends and families.

Thinking back on that conversation, I have to wonder if the poor fellow had any inkling what lay in store for his country.

He then asked if he could show me his shop where he dealt in fine Syrian art. He led me through a doorway, down some narrow, twisty stairs into a large room underground where he introduced me to his partner and proceeded to show me pictures of various sorts. I had no idea what I was buying, but figured, "What the hell, I will probably never be in a place like this again." So I bought four hand colored engravings which, my new friend told me, came from a Koran prayer book, painted in the early 1800s, beautifully done in a cartoon style. I had no idea if the $150 I paid for them might be a total rip-off or a bargain. I did bring them home, had them framed, and they still hang in my study.

Before leaving Washington I had gotten to know Abdul-Aziz Said, a Syrian and eminent professor of international relations at American University, who was most helpful to me as I prepared for the pilgrimage. He explained what I would see, gave me names of several people to look up, and otherwise filled me in on Syrian politics, culture, history, and much else. He had suggested that I visit a mosque and had arranged for a couple of his former students to pick me up and take me to one on the outskirts of Damascus.

Some sort of a prayer service was going on when we arrived;

we took off our shoes and went inside. The men in one section and women in another sat on the floor and listened to talks, said prayers, joined in singing and conversation—all about Mohammad, Islam, peace and Syria—until after midnight. Then I was escorted to a back room and introduced to Assad Ali, a distinguished looking man in his sixties—a mystic and apparently the man in charge. His carefully combed, white hair framed a friendly face; he was dressed in a flowing white robe which came to the floor, spoke perfect English, and was obviously highly educated and cultured. We had a long and animated conversation; he was a most likable and reasonable fellow, well-spoken and articulate, who appeared to be a born leader. He wanted to know who I was and why I was in Damascus; he asked from my perspective as an American how Islam appeared to differ from my Christianity.

After the events of September 11 (just three months later) and the incessant talk about Islam since, the distinction between what I saw that evening, the talks I had, and the common Western perception of Islam is surreal. Here were kind and outgoing people, busily raising their children, going to work every day or running their small businesses, as devout to their God as any good American Catholic, Protestant or Evangelical is to theirs. I recall thinking, as I looked at several hundred men spending their evening in the Mosque listening to lectures, praying, and just being present at their place of worship, that few Americans—and fewer Europeans—could be found who were as committed to their beliefs and so willing to spend the entire evening at such a gathering.

Nick and I spent the next day walking through Damascus—first down Straight Street and into the souk, then down an alley to what had once been Ananias' house, where the Apostle Paul was baptized and stayed for three days, now a chapel built right against the old city wall and marking the place where he had been let down the same wall in a basket. We were practically walking through the Scriptures. But for cars and a few modern buildings, we imagined that little had changed since Paul's times.

We came to an Orthodox Patriarchy, a beautifully kept Greek Orthodox Church being prepared for a concert. Pope John Paul II had visited there just four weeks earlier, when the same concert had been performed, in the presence of both Christians and Muslims. Nick asked an Orthodox priest there about the state of relations between the members of the two religions in Syria; he said they were excellent, that there was rarely any sort of disagreement, but that Christians and Muslims lived in a peaceful state of coexistence.

Not far away was the Citadel—also known as the Umayyad Mosque, one of the largest and most visited in the Muslim world—built around the Roman Temple of Jupiter in the first century, expanded in the third century AD on foundations built in the ninth century BC. As long as three football fields, it was used during Byzantine times as a monument to John the Baptist. Conversion by Muslims had, apparently, been rather lackluster, and many mosaics, columns, and other clearly Byzantine archi-tectural symbols are still present—at least they were in 2001. The floor inside was covered with acres of carpets, and the roof and dome soared to the sky, supported by hundreds of re-used Byzantine columns. The place is simply colossal—and often described as not only one of the great Mosques of Islam, but one of the greatest religious monuments in the world.

All of these places, at the time, seemed to me to be just more antiquities, more ancient sites, and more historical curiosities. But as we would continue our trek across Syria, visiting one after another of these Biblical sites, it became clear, in my mind, just how vast, how deep-seated, and how influential Christianity had been in this part of the world. Most of these places had been seized, at one time or another, by forces that wanted Christianity to vanish. But they would always reappear, and when they did, they would be restored or rebuilt and carefully protected and cared for by dedicated Christians.

We set off from Damascus in a rented Land Rover with a driver; we had contemplated driving ourselves, but were advised that any mishap would probably land us both in a Syrian prison. The extra $20 a day seemed like a reasonable investment, although the driver—Annas—proved to be a difficult fellow and I ultimately had to fire him and send him home.

The first stop was the third century village of Sednaya, the most holy Christian city in Syria where Aramaic, the language of Jesus, is still spoken. A nun showed us into a chapel where there hung a portrait of the Virgin Mary allegedly painted by the Apostle Luke. The portrait, the nun explained, holds special powers of healing for both Christian and Muslim young women unable to have children—prayer before it would purportedly enable them to conceive a child. And in fact, several young women sat nearby, on the floor, hoping to receive this special grace. Particularly effective, the nun told us, was for the women to stay near the painting through a night.

The icon at Sednaya had been the site of Christian miracles for centuries, and would presumably continue to be for centuries more. Soon after Muslim extremists took over that part of the country, in 2012, intent on destroying everything not to their liking, Sednaya was liquidated. According to one press report in February 2014, "the ancient monastery church and side chapels were stripped completely of their priceless religious icons and other religious objects were urinated and defecated upon. Christian villagers who were caught in the midst of the rebel assault had their throats slit, or were shot execution style at close range."

We left Sednaya and travelled to Maalula, a beautiful ancient Christian village built into a gorge just a few miles further north, with several third and fourth century churches, an orphanage, and retreat centers. Aramaic is the principal language there as well, Maalula and Sednaya being among the very few places in the world where the language is still spoken. At the top of a hill in Maalula is the monastery of St. Sergius (Mar Sarkis), named for a Roman officer who was martyred in the fourth century for refusing to renounce his Christian faith. A Catholic priest from Lebanon engaged me, in passable English, in a lengthy discussion about early Christianity—appropriately, as he told me since we were in one of the oldest extant Christian churches in the world. The semi-circular stone altar predates the Council of Nicaea (325 AD); altars after Nicaea, he explained, were rectangular. The little stone lip around the altar caught the blood of sacrificed lambs in pagan ceremonies before the birth of Christ. The little church exuded peacefulness and quiet, and I got the sense that it was timeless, and would probably remain unchanged forever.

Again, it was unfortunately not so. According to a London *Telegraph* story in 2014 Maalula was "liberated" by the Islamists; many of its inhabitants, among the few souls still speaking Aramaic, were assassinated and the rest fled. Shellfire breached the limestone walls of the ancient Christian church of Mar Sarkis and, inside, the icons—long regarded as a symbol of Syria's religious freedom—lay broken on the ground alongside crosses, catechisms, and images of the Virgin Mary.

Looking back on this pilgrimage to Syrian sites that only a few years later ceased to exist, I realize that the destruction of historical treasures in the Middle East by Islamist extremists is nothing less than a crime against civilization. News accounts do not do justice to the loss these barbarians caused as they worked their way across Syria, destroying anything that confronted their twisted outlook on the world and killing those who took a different view.

But as I reflect on these places, I tell myself that these were not the first Christians, in this part of the world, to meet such a fate, and would likely not be the last. It is said that the blood of martyrs is the seed of Christianity, and we all know that the persecution of Christians has been part of Church history since the Crucifixion. For those of us lucky enough to live in the West in these peaceful times, martyrdom is not part of our fate. Christians in the Middle East, even to this day, are not so lucky.

Our next stop was the monastery of Mar Musa (also known as the monastery of Saint Moses the Abyssinian), which sits built into a cliff a couple hundred meters above the Syrian Desert, overlooking the most forbidding land imaginable. After a strenuous hike up a very steep trail, we were welcomed by Emma, an English girl in her twenties who identified herself as an archaeologist living at the monastery—which we soon realized was not a monastery at all. Built as a Roman lookout post, it was turned into a monastery in the fifth or sixth century. Abandoned in the late nineteenth century, it was rediscovered in

1980, restored and reopened by a group of German Catholics. But by 2001 it had become something of an eclectic place, inhabited by Catholics, Greek Orthodox Christians, Eastern Rite Catholics, and even a few Protestants. Men and women were mixed together with a few semi-permanent guests. We were welcomed in, shown to a dormitory, and after a mass that was as eclectic as the guest list, served a dinner of pita bread, yoghurt, hummus, bean stew. and a bottle of wine (breakfast the next day was the just the same, as was lunch).

The man in charge—call him the abbot—was an Italian Jesuit who found the place and rebuilt it with his own money. His sidekick was a rather odd German who wandered in, was baptized, and ultimately became a monk. The place was a cross between a hippy commune with a Christian flavor and a refugio with permanent guests. After some of the serious Orthodox monasteries like Athos where we had stayed in the past, Mar Musa was an aberration.

We moved on across the desert—a lonely route, nothing on either side for miles, nary a curve in the road, and Annas insisting on driving the Land Rover as fast as it would go. I yelled at him to keep it under 130km, but after a minute or two he had it back at 165, arguing that if the speedometer said it could go that fast, that meant he should maintain 165.

Suddenly there was a crash, the car lurched into the opposite lane, and he brought it to a stop. The front left tire was completely demolished, shreds of rubber strewn down the road behind us. "No spare, no tools," confessed Annas.

But in an instant several Bedouins, robed in flowing white gowns, appeared over a little hill and surrounded the car shaking their heads. They invited us to follow them. Behind the hill we were ushered into a spacious tent with sofas and large chairs, hand woven rugs on the ground, the sort of place where you might expect to see Dean Acheson negotiating a peace treaty with a bunch of Arabs. We were offered tea and sweets while Annas was dispatched on a motorcycle to the nearest town to get a new tire and tools, and the daughters serenaded us with belly dances. Nick and I smiled at each other. "Quite a Christian retreat isn't it?" he said.

When at last our car was repaired, we headed on to the ruins of Palmyra, stately Roman columns and the remains of buildings standing proudly in the desert. The ruins were impressive: vast expanses of beautifully cut stone, the remnants of a long street lined with stone facades and pillars on both sides, and a temple 200 meters square. First built in the fourth century BC, Palmyra reached its peak in the third century AD, when it became a major trading point on the Silk Road. Although the ruins had stood there for over 2,000 years, well preserved because of the dry, hot desert climate, Islamic radicals, during the summer of 2015, blew up several of the temples, pillars and statues, including several which had no religious significance.

Remembering these places, now destroyed by Islamic terrorists, brings to the fore the contrast between peaceful Muslims—examples of which pervaded our journey—and the radical Islamists who want to destroy anything contrary to their warped beliefs. Even the Ottomans, over centuries, coexisted with the Christians in relative peace. Experiencing the coexistence of these two religions in 2001, juxtaposed to what would follow just months after our visit, made me realize that this trip to Syria gave me the opportunity to see places that future generations would never see, and the opportunity to observe Muslims and

Christians living together in relative peace that would not exist again, at least in this part of the world, during my lifetime.

From Palmyra we proceeded to the Crusader Castles. Annas was increasingly obstinate and insolent and continued to drive the Land Rover as if he was trying to win the Grand Prix. He ignored me yelling at him. But despite his determination to keep the pedal to the metal, we arrived at our first Crusader Castle in one piece.

The black, basalt crusader castle was first—vast and awe inspiring, but nothing compared to Krak des Chevaliers, which was to medieval castles what Chartres was to gothic cathedrals. Built on top of a mountain, it is a military fortress, strategically placed, built in the most massive way imaginable, and in incredibly good repair. It was occupied by Christians for over 160 years during the twelfth and thirteenth centuries without once being captured. It stands as an inspiring example of what the Crusades were about, how many people participated (tens of thousands), and their willingness to devote their lives to their mission—to God and to Christ.

Krak was described by T.E. Lawrence as "perhaps the best preserved and most wholly admirable castle in the world." We wandered through narrow passageways, up stairways wide enough to accommodate a team of horses, through tight doorways that made entry by enemies virtually impossible.

The Crusaders were an extreme form of pilgrim. To preserve Christianity, tens of thousands walked from Northern Europe to what we now call the Middle East, often in more dire circumstances than we had imagined while walking the Camino de Santiago. And when they finally arrived, to have built a fortress such as Krak—merely a couple of hours in it gives one a new admiration for the dedication of the crusaders, Christians willing to die for their faith.

Not far away we found the St. George Monastery—the oldest Christian monastery in Syria. It is a Greek Orthodox community in a medieval building, situated on a foundation from the Justinian period. We were welcomed by a young monk, given rooms, fed an ample supper, and then ushered into the chapel for an hour-long mass. Peacefulness pervaded the place. The monks were intelligent and well-educated, orderly men obviously very dedicated to their faith, and pleased to welcome a couple of westerners into their monastery.

In the morning, after a two-hour prayer service, we met with a group of Christian students visiting the monastery from a village near Homs. One young fellow sought me out; he spoke passable English, and was thrilled to find an American. Barraging me with questions about the U.S., many about all the awful things portrayed in Hollywood movies, he particularly wanted to know about freedom—something he knew we had in the U.S., but which was, he told me, in short supply in Syria. "The walls have ears, and tongues are removed for contrarian speech," he said.

I explained our perception of free speech and our freedom of religion, how it is spelled out in the First Amendment to our Constitution, and why it was put there. To Americans, I told him—or to many of us, at any rate—our freedoms are sacrosanct, the basis for the American way of life. He was amazed, and begged me to stay in touch. I gave him my email address, and he promised to write. Sadly, I never heard from him again.

The St. George Monastery was attacked and occupied by extremist Muslims in August, 2013, and several Christian soldiers were killed trying to defend it. Miraculously the building was not destroyed, but at last report the monastery was shuttered and the monks disbursed.

Our next stop was Apamea, another Roman city of astounding proportions, incredibly well preserved, but virtually deserted. We wandered down the middle of the main street, over one kilometer long, with three-story Roman and Greek building fronts on either side. The paving stones on the street were still in good shape, and there were statues standing about. We were soon approached by a shaggy looking fellow who claimed to be one of the guardians and caretakers. He took us into a tent he had pitched inside a large Roman house, gave a pot of tea to each of us, and for a few coins proceeded to give us a guided tour. He showed us mosaics—dozens of them, remarkable enough to be in the Metropolitan Museum of Art—as well as stone carvings, statues, and windows with beautiful stone partitions. We came across a theater which could still seat several hundred people: temples, churches, baths, hot and cold water systems, a row of stone toilet seats with a place for running water underneath. Everything gave the impression that with just a little work the place could again be functioning as it was a couple of hundred years after Christ.

From there it was back into the Land Rover, at breakneck speed into Aleppo, and to the Baron, probably the most famous hotel in Syria. We had no reservations—reservations were not part of our agenda—but were in luck and got a couple of rooms. By this time Nick and I decided we had had enough of Annas, and although we had hired him for the duration of the trip, decided to let him go and to continue the journey in whatever way we could devise. I was delegated to fire the man, which I did in quick dispatch; I gave him a hundred dollar bill, told him I had no time for his argument and to be on his way.

The Baron Hotel in the heart of Aleppo is a place that deserves several pages (or at least it did when we were there), but others have described it better than I. Suffice it to say that it is an anachronism, one of those 1930s-era watering holes waiting for well-dressed Englishmen to arrive and stay in style. T. E. Lawrence lived there for a year or so; Agatha Christie wrote *Murder on the Orient Express* there; Churchill visited often, as did Teddy Roosevelt, Doris Duke, and David Rockefeller, to name a few, and every other European and American of any consequence who happened to stop by Aleppo.

Main Street, Apamea, Syria

The bar could be in a Spencer Tracy movie: a large, dark-paneled room with scrubbed wooden tables, a generous selection of good whisky and gin, art deco pictures on the wall. The bartender, dressed in a perfectly starched white shirt and bow tie, white hair and beard, was the model of an old British bartender but with olive skin—the sort of Arab that you would envision serving drinks on Agatha Christie's Orient Express. As we were having a drink, a fellow approached us and introduced himself as Walid. He was apparently a fixture in the bar. In no time he struck up a conversation with us, and before the end of the evening had agreed to meet us in his 1953 Studebaker the next morning and take us on a tour of the area around Aleppo, complete with a picnic lunch and plenty to drink.

Aleppo is Syria's second largest city and claims to be one of the oldest in the world, continually inhabited for over 5,000 years. Most of those five millennia were kinder than the late twentieth century to Aleppo, which was, to say the least, a shabby mess. Robert Kaplan describes it as "a Middle Eastern version of a Communist Eastern European city, with broken windowsills, rotting doors, peeling paint and polite, seemingly exhausted people with unkempt hair and worn, baggy clothes, pushing dusty brown carts…" There were miles of narrow steers, old buildings leaning toward each other, and a colossal souk, full of every sort of Arab and Middle Eastern handicraft, cheap clothes and brass—brass by the ton, in fact.

Walid proved to be an entertaining and knowledgeable guide, who took us first to the remains of a sixth century Christian church, then on to the Saint Simeon Basilica, built in the late fifth century around a pillar where St. Simeon Stylites lived for some forty years. He supposedly wore a metal collar and chain attached to the top of the pillar to keep him from falling off, and food and other necessities were hoisted up by rope. The church was the largest church in the world when it was built, taking up some 5,000 square meters—in reality it was four churches built in the shape of a cross and all four meeting at the center point. The place was an amazing mix of columns, arches, windows, intricately carved crosses and delicate stone flowers, in amazingly good shape after 1500 years. It had become a major pilgrimage destination in the middle ages, surrounded, at the time, by shops and hostels to accommodate people from across the Middle East.

The next day we met with Professor of International Affairs at Aleppo University, Professor Elias Samo—whose name I had gotten from a friend in Washington—in a large, open-air restaurant on the central square. Samo had studied and taught at various U.S. universities and was head of the Aleppo Foreign Policy Institute. Originally from Mesopotamia, he was a Syrian Orthodox Christian, one of twenty children, and obviously well-connected and well-educated. We were joined by Samo's friend Gregorios Yohanna Ibrahim, the Syriac Orthodox Archbishop of Aleppo, a distinguished and well-spoken man in his late sixties who commanded great respect; as he walked to the table, one person after another rose to greet him—Muslims as well as Christians, not the least of which was a Muslim cleric of similar stature to the bishop. They embraced, spoke for a few minutes and shook hands before the bishop joined us. In perfect English—he had a degree from Bristol University in England—he spoke of Syrian politics, how Christianity functioned in this Muslim country and the strengths and weaknesses that it has in such a situation. In 2001 Syria was nearly one quarter

Christian; few Christians felt threatened, and, as was obvious from what we saw around us, Christians and Muslims got along well. In Syria, the Bishop told us, people of different religions live together in peace.

Twelve years after our lunch, in April 2013, while returning from Turkey with a Greek Orthodox bishop, where they had been negotiating the release of two priests who had been kidnapped a couple of months earlier, the two Bishops were kidnapped at gunpoint by radical Islamists, and their driver was shot to death. Neither has been heard from since. Before he was kidnapped, Bishop Gregorios had written that

> The plurality of religions and faiths does not foment an inter-religious conflict due to the fact that the common denominator of its teachings, heritages and ethics affirms the oneness of God and the multiplicity and integrity of its people. Whenever Christians and Muslims approach the sources of divine teaching, they may feel that their common heritage is part and parcel of the universal belief of the relationship between man (the weak) and the Creator (the mighty). Christians say we have one God and Muslim say there is no God but God.

As we drank tea after lunch on the professor's balcony, he explained just who the Assad family was and how they had come to power. They were Alawites, a sort of a bastard Shia offshoot that constituted between two and three million of Syria's twenty-two million people. Because of their minority status the Alawites needed the support of Syria's five million Christians, particularly because the country was 70 percent Sunni. His father Hafez had taught Bashar brutality—he had put down a

Sunni revolt in the city of Hama in 1982, killing 30,000 people, many of them members of the Muslim Brotherhood. Although Bashar wasn't demonstrating brutality in 2001, he certainly would as time went on.

A mini-bus took us to Homs, a gritty industrial city on the road from Aleppo to Damascus. Dirty streets lined with little shops, thousands of those concrete block apartment buildings that fill every city in the East Bloc, Asia, and the Middle East; incredible traffic going in every direction interspersed with bicycles, motorcycles and pedestrians. The al-Nassar Hotel was a fifth-floor walk-up—just the fifth floor of an apartment building—and rooms were six dollars a night, showers extra. But because we took two rooms, the shower was thrown in for free. The clerk, a man in his seventies who learned English building pipelines across the desert for ARAMCO in the 1950s, explained that we could use the Arab toilets for free, but the western toilet was 50 cents extra—the best 50 cents I spent on the entire trip.

Perhaps the best thing Homs had to offer was the bus station, a place of total chaos which somehow worked—an example of a bottom-up enterprise with nobody in charge. There were at least 100 minibuses waiting in no apparent order, no signs to indicate where they were going or when. Somehow we found the bus to Baalbek in Lebanon and squeezed into the furthest back seat; there were at least fifteen people in a vehicle built for twelve, all somewhat amazed to find an American and a Brit among them. We were offered oranges and whatever anybody had as we chugged along, across the border into Lebanon and to Baalbek.

Our stopping point, the Palmyra Hotel, was another trip into the 1930s. The grand hotel of this old tourist destination was built in the 1870s at the height of the age of the European grand tour, and boasted that it has never closed its doors since—not even for one day. Kaiser Wilhelm stayed there in 1898; the German general staff occupied it during World War I and the Americans during World War II.

The hotel was just a stone's throw from Jupiter's Temple, Baalbek's principle attraction. Built shortly before the birth of Christ, the Roman Emperor Augustus decided to build the grandest and mightiest temple of antiquity in the middle of nowhere—nowhere being Baalbek. Built over the course of 250 years, it remains one of the great examples of Imperial Roman architecture and construction. Pilgrims thronged to the sanctuary to honor three deities: Jupiter, Venus, and Mercury. Its courtyard is retained by three walls containing twenty-seven limestone blocks, unequaled in size anywhere in the world, weighing some 300 metric tons each. The place is as large as St. Peter's in Rome.

As we were checking out of the Palmyra we struck up a conversation with Edmund Khoury, a Lebanese Christian who ran an English-speaking K-12 international school in Beirut and who kindly offered to give us a lift back to Damascus. He was full of information about Damascus, the politics and the culture, the Muslims, the Alawites and the Christians and how they all fit together—all in relative harmony, he said, at least for now. But he warned that the extremist Muslims were sure to come to Syria and that the relative peace would not last for long.

It is hard to imagine, in light of our seemingly peaceful and educational pilgrimage, just what has transpired in Syria since. The total destruction of Aleppo—it is said that it took 4,000 years to build it and only four to destroy—the killing of hundreds of thousands of innocent civilians, the devastation to Christian heritage sites, the millions of people whose homes and lives were destroyed and are displaced or in camps in the Turkish desert. The virtual destruction of an entire culture is a vivid reminder of the slim reed that separates civilization from nihilism and devastation. As I look back on my memories of the places I was privileged to visit before they were destroyed, I wonder: what other places might be next?

6

THE PAINTED CHURCHES OF BUCOVINA, ROMANIA

June 2007

WE DID NOT TAKE A TRIP for several years after Syria for a number of reasons—mostly personal on both of our parts— but then, it was not as if we had some grand scheme for these pilgrimages with a plan or schedule. As mentioned earlier, our travels together were all a very spontaneous enterprise.

Nick had a colleague who had visited a very remote part of Romania that was both interesting and beautiful but particularly fascinating because it had several very old churches painted on the outside—the "Painted Churches of Bucovina" as they were called. I thought it might be worthwhile to go there on what would be the sixth of our pilgrimages. By 2007, I was ready to go off again, and had always been particularly interested in Romania because of a book that I had published earlier.

This would be the first of several trips into the former East Bloc—the Communist Warsaw Pact countries that had been freed in the late 1980s. I had visited several before, and in fact had been to Romania in the late '90s, and was anxious to go back to find out how these places, and particularly their faith, were emerging from Communist oppression. Romania was largely an Orthodox country; as I studied its history from World War II on, I learned that although the Church had been suppressed, there were areas—Bucovina being one of them—where Christianity was coming back.

Romania had been the last of the East Bloc countries to emerge from Communism, and its emergence had been the only violent overthrow. The country had been ruled by the awful Nicolae Ceaușescu and his equally horrible wife, Elena. A counter-revolution had developed in December 1989, and the Ceaușescu s were seized, given a quick military trial, sentenced to death, and executed on Christmas Day, 1989.

I arrived in Bucharest to find it improved since I had last been there, ten years earlier, but it was still Bucharest—miles of those miserable concrete apartment buildings found from one end of the former Soviet Bloc to the other, skinny dogs looking for a morsel of food and funny little three-cylinder cars spewing black smoke as they careened around the city. The people looked like a cross between southern Italians and South Americans, speaking a sort of Mediterranean language that was actually closer to ancient Latin than to modern Italian or Spanish. The place was an original mix, according to writer and traveller Robert Kaplan: "...a population that looked Italian but wore the expressions of Russian peasants; an architectural backdrop that often evoked France and Central Europe; and service and physical conditions that resembled those in Africa."

But the sky was blue, the air was warm and the grass and trees were green as could be on the Sunday afternoon in June that I arrived at Otopeni, Bucharest's airport. Nick would be along later in the evening, coming from London, so I had a few hours to wander through Bucharest, get a leisurely lunch, and find out how things had changed since the collapse of communism eighteen years earlier.

After a walk through old Bucharest, such as it was, and visits to a couple of crowded churches, we caught the noon train to Iasi (pronounced "Yash"), the provincial capital of Moldavia. The train was passable—sort of like the lowest class and slowest train in Western Europe in the 1950s, even though it was the fast train and we were in first class. It was, however, a vast improvement over the last first class Romanian train I had been on in 1993, going from Bucharest to Timisoara, Sighisoara, Cluj, and on to Budapest, which was so decrepit and filthy that you would have thought you were in the depths of the poorest country in Africa. It was pouring rain and water literally came through every crack in the car. The lights didn't work, and the toilet was a sort of hole in the floor with a porcelain bowl above it, no seat or other accouterments, the ties rushing by below.

Fortunately, conditions were somewhat better on the train Nick and I took from Bucharest. Six hours later, after what seemed like a stop about every eight kilometers, we arrived in Iasi, the most important city in Moldavia and the city which appears more often than any other in Romanian history. Moldavia is just west of Moldova, with its northern border lying against Ukraine—which is practically within sight of Iasi. Moldova was the only remaining communist country in

Europe in 2002; it had gained independence in 1989 with the disintegration of the Soviet Bloc, but the communists returned to power, after riots and demonstrations, in 2001. We had been warned not to wander over the border.

Moldavia had once been part of Moldova, but was absorbed by Romania in 1859, and has remained a Romanian province, more or less, ever since. It has been known as a hotbed of Romanian nationalism, and Iasi had actually served as the Romanian capital after the Germans captured Bucharest during World War I.

Our guidebook told us that there was a monastery with a guesthouse that would welcome pilgrims, which we eventually found, after walking from church to church, winding up at the great Orthodox Cathedral, built in 1833, which sat on the side of a hill overlooking what looked like an industrial wasteland. The Metropolitan, or head man in the Orthodox hierarchy, directed us to the guesthouse, where we were given two clean and attractive rooms. This was the first of several such places we would find over the next couple of weeks as we wandered through the Moldavian countryside.

Iasi was a vibrant mix between old European charm and Soviet-style buildings, small shops, and post-Soviet smoke-laden heavy industry, all interspersed with many busy churches. It was badly destroyed in World War II during fierce fighting between German and Soviet forces, but few signs of destruction remained.

On my early morning walk I was surprised to find a Mass just getting underway in a large Roman Catholic Church. The place was nearly full, and most of the worshipers were peasant-looking Romanians who regarded me—obviously neither a peasant nor a Romanian—as a curiosity. But they were more concerned with the Mass than they were with me. I had converted to Catholicism a couple of years earlier, after a long period agonizing about it, and was pleased to find a Mass in such a remote place.

Although Romania is for all intents and purposes an Orthodox country, about 15 percent of the population is Catholic and 3 to 4 percent is Protestant. Before World War II there was a sizable Jewish population, but most were either killed by the Romanian Iron Guard, Nazis, or emigrated to neighboring Poland and Czechoslovakia. Iasi itself was nearly a third Jewish before the war; because of its proximity to the Russian border, Jews had fled Russian persecutions for centuries. In 1941, as a diversionary tactic, and because the Jews were thought to be aiding the Soviet Union, Romanian and German soldiers launched a pogrom and killed nearly half of the Jewish population, the largest massacre of Jews in Romania. The rest either fled or were persecuted and killed over the remainder of the war. There had once been well over a hundred synagogues, but we found only one—a run-down, locked, and overgrown little stone building.

There were no trains or buses, so we hired a driver to take us to the convent at Agapia, about a three-hour drive which we made in less than two at breakneck speed. Ion, our driver, spoke enough English to be a fount of information on the history, culture, and politics of Moldova, and it was our good fortune that he was something of an expert on the painted churches we were about to visit. Ion was a great admirer of Stephen the Great, one of Romania's most beloved kings, who had defeated the Turks during the fifteenth century, according to Ion, and had ordered that forty-four churches be built in Moldova—one for each of the battles with the Turks that he had won. All were built in a unique style, and King Stephen had ordered that they be painted on the outside with frescos. We would learn much more about these churches over the next several days.

We were welcomed into Agapia by two friendly nuns. They assured us that we could stay for as long as we liked for a minimal charge; they would feed us and they urged us to pray with them and make ourselves at home. My room looked out onto a garden full of red and yellow flowers, tangled vines of honeysuckle and trumpet vine growing on trellises, all full of birds singing and chirping at the top of their lungs. To understand Agapia, the nuns told us, we'd need to start with old Agapia, the original monastery situated a mile or so up the mountain. Virtually inaccessible by road, we were led by our new friends, dressed in their flowing habits and hiking boots, up a muddy road, across a stream and up a steep valley to Agapia on the Hill, a convent of about forty nuns. This was the original monastery, first built in 1527, and, as the facility was outgrown, expanded at the beginning of the seventeenth century to Agapia in the Valley, where we would stay. Little appeared to have changed since 1527, although the small buildings were well-preserved and clean, the paintings on the wall in amazingly good shape. The nuns were particularly proud of their flowers—incredible gardens overflowing with every colored flower imaginable. The monastery had originally been built for monks, but became a convent for nuns in the early nineteenth century.

Back at the lower facility, one of the nuns showed us around, first to the church—the center, of course, of the whole operation, built in 1647 and dedicated to the Archangels Michael and Gabriel—then through the rest of the buildings, to the gardens and fields, and to the workshops. Agapia is a self-supporting place, known particularly for its embroidery and carpets, and is inhabited by over 500 nuns. The main building, built of white stucco, surrounds a courtyard on all four sides, with a balcony, looking into the courtyard and supported by wood pillars, which went all the way around. The convent had been attacked and robbed repeatedly over its nearly 500 year's existence, but the courtyard was built to be impenetrable and had kept both nuns and villagers safe from attackers. During the communist years, the enterprising nuns had woven carpets used in Ceaușescu 's wedding-cake palace in Bucharest, and thus had been allowed to live in relative peace—something few of the other monasteries that we would be visiting could say. "We were lucky that we had something that Ceaușescu wanted," the nuns explained. Most of the other monasteries had been closed, or at least shuttered during the communist period, and those that survived did so surreptitiously, only getting away with it because they were so far off the beaten path.

The monasteries and convents grow much of their own food on farms scattered throughout the valley. The nuns and monks do all the work, mostly with horses and by hand, and an occasional small tractor. It is not unusual to see a four-wheel hay wagon, piled high with loose hay and pulled by a team of horses and driven by a nun, habit and all. The June hay was in full harvest, the nuns and monks were busily cutting hay with scythes, pulling it with a team of horses and a chain into piles, and lifting it with pitchforks onto haystacks, secured with poles which they bound onto the top to form a protective cover from the winds and rain—a process unchanged since medieval times. Most of the nuns came from small towns and farms, and were not only dedicated to God but very practical as well. I commented to one how kind they were to put us up, to feed us, show us around, and so on. "It is just part of our service to God," she explained.

Orthodoxy has always had a very strong monastic tradition, originating in the second century after Christ. The monks consider themselves called by Christ to remove themselves from the world of laymen—to be in the world, but not of the world, as set forth in the Gospel of John (17:13-16). They set the moral standards for all Christians, taking vows of chastity, poverty, celibacy, and prayer, and are self-sufficient in their daily lives. The Moldavian monks and nuns differed greatly from those we had met several years earlier on Mt. Athos in Greece. With cars, electricity, farms where they raised cattle and hogs, and with their craft shops where they made commercially marketable goods like carpets, embroidery, furniture and metal works, they were part of the world, whereas the Athos monks were almost as far removed from everyday life as they could be and still be in Europe.

Agapia is in the depths of Bucovina—our destination, translated as "beech-covered land"—and truly one of the forgotten corners of Europe. Its history is brutal; most recently it was part of Romania, which fought with the Germans until 1943 when it was captured by Stalin, but only after the Iron Guard, Romania's answer to the SS, had murdered virtually all of the Jews. It was then turned over to the ruthless Romanian Communists, only to be liberated with the fall of Ceauşescu in 1989. Sachaverell Sitwell, the brother of Dame Edith and Sir Osbert, who travelled there in the early years of World War II, wrote that "in no other district that I have ever visited, be it in Spain or Portugal, in Sweden or the Gaeltacht of Western

Ireland, is there this sensation of remoteness…. a land of green meadows and firewood. It is at an inconceivable distance from newspaper and tram." Bucovina reminded me of the Black Forest in Germany in the 1950s, where I had spent a year at a boarding school in 1957—then a bucolic and unspoiled mountainous region with the occasional timbered farmhouse, teams of oxen and horses pulling hay-laden wagons and tanks full of stinking liquid manure making their way down narrow windy roads. Bucovina still had nearly as many horse-drawn wagons as trucks, loaded with everything from hay to newly made pine furniture, driven by sturdy peasants with bright checkered shirts and sheepskin vests, their wives and children riding alongside. The green pastures would poke up into the steep mountain forests like fingers. The air was clean and fresh, the roads uncrowded, without any of those dreadful broken-down Romanian factories to be seen.

I awoke early the next morning to the sound of a mallet tapping on wood. One of the nuns was balancing a long beam on one shoulder, tapping out a call to prayer. During the siege of Moldova by the Ottomans in the fourteenth and fifteenth centuries the Turks forbade the use of bells so the monasteries instead started using wooden beams and mallets, and the tradition endured. The beam was dark wood which looked like walnut, tapered at both ends, and smooth from thousands of pairs of hands holding it.

I quickly dressed and met Nick in the hall and we went to the chapel to join the nuns in their early morning prayers. Orthodox churches have no seats or pews, only places to stand (it discourages day dreaming) and after an hour of listening to their sing-song prayers my feet were ready for a break and my stomach ready for breakfast. Fortunately, a meal was waiting for us.

Afterwards, one of the nuns insisted on driving us—in the monastery's van used to take nuns back and forth to their distant fields—first to the monastery at Neamt and then on to the town of Targu Neamt, which had been, until 1945, largely a Jewish community. It maintained its typically Romanian atmosphere of timbered houses and crooked streets, the Carpathian Mountains rising nearby.

We decided to walk from there to the Voronet monastery, which was down a beautiful poplar-lined country road about ten kilometers outside of town, heavily travelled by farmers with their horses going to and from their fields, a scene one could expect to see in pre–World War II Germany. The horse-drawn, rubber-tired wagons would emerge through breaks in the poplars with freshly cut hay stacked twelve feet high or more and would slowly lumber along, the horses straining to pull them along the road, their drivers coaxing them. A stream flowed fifty feet or so below the level of the road, where I notice a farmer who had driven his horse and wagon down a path to the river, and had filled the wagon with round river rock, stacked up as high as the little sides on the wagon. The poor horse, skinny and apparently tired from a day's work, strained to pull the wagon, loaded with a ton or so of rock, up the embankment. His owner stood behind the poor beast with a whip, lashing it across the back with all his strength. I wanted to run over and restrain the man, but thought better of it when I considered that I might easily become the victim of the whip. It seemed to me typically Romanian—never would one find such a scene in France, Italy, Germany, or Spain or anywhere else in Europe. But if Ceaușescu had taught the world anything, it was that

Romanians must have a streak of cruelty running through them.

The Romanians call Voronet the Sistine Chapel of the East, and for good reason. Built in 1488, it is one of the most stunning of all the painted monasteries. Hundreds of frescos cover the inside and outside walls; scenes from the Old and New Testaments, lives of the early saints, and pictures of early church history cover every square inch. The favored color is a vivid blue, known, surprisingly, as "Voronet blue." The composition of the paint, in one of those ancient mysteries that modern science cannot unravel, remains unknown. As do many of the monasteries, Voronet's frescos include the Tree of Jesse, a depiction of the ancestry of Jesus inspired by a passage in the Book of Isaiah: "There shall come forth a shoot from the stem of Jesse, and a branch shall grow out of his roots." The New Testament begins, in the Book of Matthew, with the genealogy of Christ, which recounts that Jesse "begat David the king" who begat Solomon and on to Joseph and then Jesus. The Jesse Tree has been a favorite subject for Christian art since the middle ages, in all sorts of variations, forms, and styles. Voronet may be unique, however, as its Tree of Jesse contains images of several Greek philosophers, including Aristotle and Plato.

Stephen the Great ruled Moldavia from 1457 to 1504. Constantinople had fallen to the Turks just four years before he was crowned, and the Ottoman Empire was on a rampage through Europe until its final defeat, at Vienna, in 1683. Stephen, who was a great warrior and a devout Christian, resisted the Islamic invasion in battle after battle, and built the Bucovina churches in celebration after each of his victories over the forces of the East. The style was an elegant, octagonal steeple raised on a tall, star-shaped base. Frescoes were used before

Stephen built these churches, and many traditional Byzantine churches in Greece, Serbia, and Bulgaria often had frescos on the outside as well as the inside. But as the Moldavian peasants were mostly illiterate, Stephen wanted the churches to be places where the peasants could learn the stories in the Bible. His solution was to have murals painted on the outside walls of the churches representing complete cycles of religious stories and the lives of the Orthodox saints—sort of religious cartoons understandable to the villagers. Miraculously, the artists used paints that not only survived the elements, even to this day, but which maintained their vivid colors as well.

These monasteries were literally overflowing with young monks and nuns, unlike monasteries in Western Europe. I wanted to know why this was and thought somebody in this monastery might be able to give some idea. So we sought out the abbot, who was most receptive and anxious to answer our questions. I asked him what was going on in this remote corner of Romania, where just twenty years earlier all religion was mocked and practically illegal, where most of the monasteries had been shuttered, or at best operated on the sly, where the only monks were born before 1940. What was it about this place, I asked him, that attracted so many young people who were willing to give up everything, to take a vow of poverty, to abandon twenty-first century modernity to join a monastery?

The abbot explained, in broken but understandable English, that this was a natural response to the excesses of the Communist state that Romania had so recently been. The repressive Ceaușescu regime had tried to wipe out individuality, had imposed a police state that spied on everything and everybody, and that tried to make everybody suspicious of everybody else. When it was suddenly overthrown in 1989 and Romania became a somewhat normal sort of place again, Orthodox Christianity blossomed forth like wildflowers in the forest in the spring, he explained. Old churches were rebuilt and new ones built from the ground up and families flocked to them. Bibles were printed and studied, Christianity was taught in schools, and thousands of young men and women joined the monasteries and convents. It was a phenomenon unlike anything else going on in the Christian world. Under communism, official religion was just a part of the secular state. Now, official religion gave people something substantive to believe in.

"How does one go about becoming a monk?" I asked the abbot.

"Candidates choose a monastery where they think they'd like to join," he explained, "and come and stay for a week or so, working, eating, and praying with us. When they are satisfied that we are the right place, they join as novices for three years. During that time, they can decide if the monastic life is right for them, and we can decide if we think they would fit in here and would make good monks." Not much different from the discernment process we had heard about on Mt. Athos and in France.

The next morning it was pouring rain. We had planned to walk to Moldovita, but caught a taxi instead, and arrived at a small village surrounding a fortified quadrangle, complete with gates and a tower, and a beautiful church at its center, covered with painted frescoes. Moldovita was built in 1535 and was well preserved; the paintings were fresh-looking and flowers bloomed everywhere. Here the dominant color was yellow; the paint was made, we were told, from the sulphur in the adjacent hills and really came alive when hit by the sun—but not today, as the rain continued. The buildings were all of handsome stone surrounded by carefully tended grass and small flower gardens.

A smiley nun, wearing a plastic rain coat over her habit, took us in tow and showed us around. She spoke a little French which quickly became the common language between us—it was not clear whether hers or mine was worse, but we seemed to understand each other well enough. On one outside wall she pointed out a large fresco of the defense of Constantinople in 626 AD against Persians who looked, she said, more like Turks than Persians. In fact, the artists had no idea what seventh century Persians looked like, and so used contemporary Turks as the models instead—having fought battle after battle against them, they knew exactly, she said with a little laugh, knew just what Turks looked like and assumed that nobody would know the difference. She then took us around to the front door, where there was a depiction of the Last Judgment. All the paintings are original, she told us; the colors were as vivid as could be, both on the inside and outside walls, with the exception of the north walls on the outside, where the paint was faded and the pictures less clear. Not surprising after 460 years!

Wealthy families and rulers in Romania maintained a tradition of building churches and monasteries in their villages and endowing them with forest, farmlands, vineyards, and even entire villages. These families would give them paintings, statues, and other valuables—a practice that continued long after their founding. Typically throughout the Balkans, monasteries were built in the form of a fortress, complete with stone wall and fortified gates, with a church in the middle where it would be safe from invading armies and thieves. Inside the walls were everything that the monks and nuns, as well as the villagers, would need for months at a time, including workshops, storage bins full of grain and food, fresh water and firewood.

The frescos of the painted churches were mostly done by local artists, who often had outside help from travelling professional artisans. The Bucovina climate required that artists know how to make paint and apply it to the plaster so that it could not be quickly washed away. Spring and fall is a time of continual rain, and winters can be brutally cold with meters of snow and ice accompanied by violent winds from the steppes. Art historians have always marveled at the way these outside frescos survived such brutal weather. It was thought for years that the paint was made with egg yolk and that the fatty substances withstood the water, ice and snow. But recent tests have determined that the rich colors are strictly the product of local minerals, and that trial and error resulted in their use. The reds, we now know, came from ocher extracted from iron oxide clays, and blue pigments from unstable copper carbonate and from lapis lazuli, while greens were made from copper carbonate and yellows from clay rich in iron oxide and from sulphur. Pigments were mixed with lamp-black or charcoal so as to counteract the absorbent nature of plaster on which they were painted.

Whatever they did, they did it well, as the paint is often still as vivid as if applied yesterday. The images were clear, lines were definite, and the colors bright.

We had asked the taxi driver to wait, since the rain didn't seem to slow down in the slightest, and had him drive us on to Sucevita. All of the painted monasteries are within fifteen or twenty kilometers of each other, usually either up narrow mountain trails or along windy, mountain roads. Given the rain, we were relieved to be inside a taxi. Sucevita was the last of the Bucovina painted monasteries, built in 1581, and the walls and defensive towers surrounding the monastery are still intact. Like many of the others, Sucevita has extraordinarily broad eaves to protect the frescos from the weather—or some of it. Its prize painting is a depiction of the ladder of paradise: a slanted ladder, each rung inscribed with monastic qualities— silence, obedience, virtue—reaches to heaven, with rows of red-winged angels attending to the righteous, while the wicked fall through the rungs to be met by grinning devils, who push them into the chaos that is hell. Good and evil were certainly more distinguished in the sixteenth century than they are in our post-modern culture. No moral relativism and not much left to the imagination—and certainly little doubt as to how the Ceauşescu 's and their henchmen would have fared.

Our next destination was the little town of Radauti, 17 kilometers down a relatively flat, straight, and uncommonly busy road. After a bite of lunch we set off on foot along the road, still in the rain, hoping that we might hitch a ride or that some other good luck would come along. It didn't take long until we were both soaked, and after about 15 kilometers of trudging along the highway, rain beating on us, being splashed each time a truck or car went by, good luck finally prevailed and a farmer stopped and beckoned us to hop aboard his horse drawn wagon. We proceeded at a full trot, rain continuing to find its way into every crack and button hole that wasn't already soaked. The horse was called "Doro" the farmer told us, which amused me, as the only other Doro I had ever met was George W. Bush's only sister, who receded out of sight soon after Bush was elected. But Doro did get us into town, and there we found the only hotel which, thanks be to God, had a room for us, where we proceeded to dry out our stuff and ourselves. We stopped in the dining room to have a drink of wine before going upstairs, and were the only ones in a very deserted place. When we came back down a couple of hours later we found the place packed with locals drinking beer and clustered around a small black and white television set, watching the World Cup soccer tournament. Here in this far off little place, halfway round the world, these young men, settled into a tavern watching the World Cup, probably had about the same sentiments as would a bunch of Chicagoans watching the same game in their home town or anywhere else in the world.

Putna, near to Radauti, is perhaps the most famous and one of the largest of the Bucovina painted monasteries, and the first built by Stephen—and the site of Stephen's tomb. No painting decorates the outside, but the inside walls are nevertheless covered with images, faces, and scenes from the New Testament. The place is inhabited by seventy monks who farm and make icons to support themselves. Nearby, several hundred yards above the front gate, a white cross sticks up from above the spruce trees. Legend has it that Stephen came upon the little valley where Putna now sits and, in order to find just the right spot for the church, climbed the hill—marked by the white cross—overlooking the place and shot three arrows. The first would determine the site of the monastery's well, the second the altar of the church he would build, and the third the site of the bell tower.

As we came in the front gate we were met by a pleasant young man who told us he was one of the artists restoring the frescos inside the bell tower, and when he figured out that I was an American and Nick a Brit, he practically dragged us into the bell tower, past a sign which undoubtedly said "no entry" in

Romanian, up four flights of precarious scaffolding, all in almost pitch black, to the top of the bell tower. He burst into a little well-lit room and introduced us to his uncle.

Monastery at Putna, Bukovina, Romania

Mihai Morosan spoke enough English that we could have a learned and intelligent conversation, and told us that he was a well-renowned church artist, had restored paintings in churches from Greece to Helsinki, England, and the U.S., and was now in charge of restoring the frescoes at Putna. He was right out of central casting: a short and stubby little man of sixty-five or so, a great shock of white hair with a handle-bar mustache and sideburns that went well below his jaw.

His work was fantastic; he was recreating the frescos of the sixteenth century as they had been painted 500 years earlier. He showed us photos of work he had done in Northern Europe, in Italy, in the Holy Land, and elsewhere. Each was as close to the original as what he was doing in Putna. What a treat, I thought to be in the presence of such a fantastic artist, somebody who could go to any part of the Christian world and recreate the best of the art that had been such a great part of the Christian tradition. He had been hired by the abbot of Putna, with some money received from the Romanian government, to repair frescos on the inside of the bell tower that had been damaged by years of neglect. If there had ever been a stairway up the tower it was gone, and had been replaced by scaffolding built by local carpenters out of saplings lashed together with rope after it had been discovered that there were actually paintings high on the inside walls. Mihai explained that Putna was the first monastery built by Stephen, between 1466 and 1481, and is one of the few without paintings on the outside. Mihai was convinced that because the bell tower had a special place in Stephen's heart, having been the target of one of his arrows, he had biblical scenes painted inside. According to the booklets available at the Putna Monastery, Stephen only later had thought of painting the outside of the churches.

Mihai's clothes were covered with every color of paint, his hands gnarled and cracked. English was only one of his languages, and when he learned where we were from he decided that we deserved a coffee, and led us down the four flights of steep and treacherous ladders to his apartment just inside the walls of the monastery.

I asked whether he had the resources to do what needed

to be done. "The paint," he told me, "is not adequate. They will only give me paint made in Romania, and it does not have the consistency I need to paint on 500-year-old plaster. I need paint made in America or Germany but cannot get it." To my inexperienced eyes it looked fine—what he was doing looked to me the way the walls must have looked in 1481. But, I thought to myself, maybe I can help. I would see if I could either get somebody to help support his effort, or even send some paint for him after I returned home.

He lived in Suceva, he told us, and travelled back and forth every three or four days in his Audi, which was incongruously sitting just outside the door. His apartment was straight out of the set of *The Agony and the Ecstasy*—paints everywhere, drawings of the Virgin Mary and the Christ child sketched on the plaster walls, canvases stretched on easels and art books strewn about the place as if a hurricane had just gone through. After a cup of very strong coffee, Mihai took us to meet the Abbott who, after a brief conversation, served us a first class breakfast and showed us through the monastery museum, full of relics from Putna, medieval manuscripts, and the Bible that Stephen always carried into battle against the Turks.

We told Mihai that we'd be in Suceva later in the week and would be flying back to Bucharest from there. "Come to see me at my house," he urged us. "Come have dinner with me and my wife and children." He gave us his telephone number, and then saw to it that we were given rooms in the guest house just outside the walls and roared off in his Audi to Suceva. Several days later, we arrived in Suceva and spent the afternoon in his comfortable apartment with his wife and son—an apartment full of religious artwork and statues and lined with books. Again the conversation turned to the paints and fine brushes he could not get in Romania.

When I returned to Washington I appealed to a large foundation—I knew the director quite well—which I knew to be interested in European architectural preservation and religious issues, to see if I could prevail on them to make a grant to the Putna monastery to refurbish the paintings. Alas, they would not, so I ordered a collection of the paints and brushes that Mihai so badly wanted and had them sent off to Suceva.

About an hour's walk from Putna we discovered what must be one of the most unique sites in Europe. Putna itself could accommodate no more monks, so the monks had raised money from local residents and were building a second monastery. In few other places in the Western world is there a new monastery being built from the ground up. A small chapel, built in the Moldavian style, complete with frescos on the inside and outside, was already finished. The smell of fresh wood beams and fresh plaster and the sun shining through leaded windows must have been what Putna was like 500 years ago. A much larger church, large enough for a couple hundred souls, was under construction, and several other buildings were finished. There were, so far, about forty monks who had signed on; one of them, who spoke English, took us under his wing and proudly showed us the workshops, where monks were diligently crafting woodworks, icons, and tapestries; to the kitchen and pantries, where the grains, vegetables, and meats grown on the monastery's farms were processed and stored; to the library and, of course, most important of all, to the new churches. The monks were inordinately proud of the place and of the workmanship that had gone into building it, and proud of the villagers and surrounding farmers who had donated the money. In 1989, when the communist government was overthrown, nobody in Romania, with the exception of the corrupt government officials, had any money. Now, not even twenty years later, people had saved enough that they could donate sufficient funds for a new monastery to be built. I wondered if American villagers and farmers would be so generous.

The Orthodox monks were almost always friendly, respectful, and anxious to talk about the West, about Communism and how things had changed, about their lives as monks and even about how their beliefs might have differed from ours. At least, they were almost always friendly, but there were exceptions. Orthodoxy sometimes has a way of being rigid and strict in one's attitudes and of being unforgiving of other Christians—an attitude we did, on occasion, encounter. I recall a lengthy and rather unpleasant conversation with a young and very bright monk at Putna who, when Nick (dressed in short pants, a t-shirt, and hiking boots) mentioned he was an Anglican scholar, had no hesitation lighting into him with a vengeance. No self-respecting theologian could possibly be dressed in such a way and be true to his faith, we were told. His opinion of Anglicanism was only slightly higher than his opinion of Nick's clothing, and each low opinion seemed to reinforce the other. There simply were no defenses—he was right and we were wrong, and that was the end of it.

After a couple of days in and around Putna we decided to walk, through the woods, about 20 kilometers back to Sucevita, the monastery where we had been a few days earlier. Our guidebook included a route and description of the trail, which sounded easy enough. But since the book had been written things had changed; some logging was being done, the trails were poorly marked, if marked at all, and after 10 kilometers or so we were hopelessly lost. But it was a beautiful, clear June day, the terrain was spectacular—steep hills covered with spruce trees, deep valleys, rushing streams and not a soul in sight—and after at least 20 kilometers we eventually came to the road leading to Sucevita. We were exhausted by this time and stopped to ask a man working in his garden if he knew how we could find a ride to the next town, another 25 or so kilometers away. Transfixed by the phenomenon of suddenly having an American and a Brit at his disposal, he said he would drive us there, but first invited us into his garden, saw that we were comfortable, brought us cold bottles of beer, bread and fresh fruit, and sat down to talk. He introduced himself as Iosef. He had been a helicopter mechanic in Ceaușescu's air force and had flown with the group that assassinated Ceaușescu and his wife in 1989. Later, as he drove us into town, I asked if he had ever heard of my friend Ian Mihai Pacepa.

One of the first major books that I had published, when I got into book publishing in the 1980s, was *Red Horizons*, the account of what actually went on inside Ceaușescu's government by Ian Mihai Pacepa, Ceaușescu's chief of foreign intelligence, who had defected to the United States several years earlier. Pacepa was the highest-ranking Soviet bloc intelligence officer ever to defect to the West, and his story was only slightly less sensational than were the consequences of his defection and subsequent publication of his book. After we published it in 1987, the book was released in more than twenty other countries, received major publicity around the world, and was ultimately read aloud, on Radio Free Europe, into Romania, where most Romanians who had radios listened to every word at the risk of being shot. The book was rebroadcast in late 1989, which apparently was one of the instigators of the demonstrations and ultimate overthrow of the regime and assassination of Mr. and Mrs. Ceaușescu on Christmas Day, 1989. Pacepa became something of a folk hero to most Romanians as a result.

"Heard of him?" Iosef responded. "Have I heard of him? Of course, everybody in Romania has heard of him. He is one of the bravest Romanians of recent times. He is one of our heroes. And how, my dear American friend, do you know of him?"

When I told him I was his publisher, he nearly drove off the road. What good fortune had befallen him, he asked, that Pacepa's American publisher had wound up sitting in his living room drinking a cold beer, and was now in the backseat of his car? He had read *Red Horizons*, but then everybody in Romania had read it. "Pacepa exposed the monster, the vampire and his vampire wife to us," Iosef explained. "After we listened to *Red Horizons* on Radio Free Europe, it was inevitable that he would be overthrown."

Iosef dropped us in the middle of the little town of Gura Humorlui, bid us farewell, and drove off. He may be still telling people about meeting Pacepa's publisher.

Ceaușescu 's Romania was among the most repressive Communist bloc countries. Ceaușescu and his family lived like kings while the rest of the country lived in poverty and near starvation. The Securitate—the secret police—were ruthless and all-powerful, spied on everybody virtually all the time, and imprisoned tens of thousands of political prisoners for years at a time. Ceaușescu had many towns across Romania bulldozed to make way for factories and concrete block apartment buildings and moved thousands upon thousands of peasants, many of whom had lived on the same farms and the same villages for generations, into those apartments so that they could work twelve to fourteen hours a day in the factories. But Bucovina had escaped such madness, and the villages still looked much as they had before World War I. Gura Humorlui was such a place—small and quiet, quaint but very Eastern European, the streets lined with timbered houses, flower boxes in the windows full of red geraniums and neat little gardens in front, a small river running through the middle of town, all surrounded by steep, heavily forested mountains. The town had been part of the Austro-Hungarian Empire until 1918, and by that time had a large Jewish population, all of whom were deported or killed by the Romanian Iron Guard before and during World War II.

Incongruously, the most imposing building on the central square was a Best Western Hotel, one of the few virtues of which was that one could get a good shot of bourbon at its bar. We consulted our guidebook, which suggested that we try to stay at a little B&B not far from the center of town, so we made our way to the Pension Christian, to find that indeed two rooms were available. Constantin, our host, was a friendly man who spoke some English which, he told us, he had learned while working in the foreign office. Of course, the Communist period was high on his list of topics of conversation, and before long, without any idea who I was, he brought up Pacepa. He had a well-tattered copy of *Red Horizons*, in Romanian, on his shelf which he quickly got down and had me autograph. After a bottle of Romanian wine and much conversation, he insisted that we join him and his family for a sumptuous dinner; when we were done, his son, not more than fourteen, played Beethoven sonatas and Chopin etudes on the piano—as well as any fourteen-year-old I had ever heard play.

Before leaving the next morning, Constantin showed us his ultimate pride and joy: his rose garden. He proudly told us that he had over 100 varieties of roses, which he had planted in a beautifully laid out and cared for garden next to his house. He knew the name of each, where it came from, when it had been planted. He knew every size rose, every color, and had carefully labeled each of them; I had never seen such an extravagant home garden before, or met anybody who cared so much for God's creation. Constantin's garden was a fitting farewell to Bucovina.

The trip taught me several unanticipated lessons. Perhaps most important, it was clear that the Romanian people—at least those in Bukovina—not unlike their painted churches, had maintained their identity and their dignity through one of the most brutal dictatorships of modern times. Communist Romania was one of the most oppressive regimes in the East Bloc, and Nicolae Ceaușescu one of the most heartless and inhumane heads of state. As the painted churches have survived hundreds of years through rain, sleet, and snow, so too did the peasants and others survive the brutality of an oppressive communist regime and emerge with their faith intact and freedom once again restored, ready to rehabilitate the churches and monasteries that were so much a part of their lives.

As I thought of those brave people, I could not get Mihai the painter out of my mind. He may have exemplified the rebuilding of the Romanian culture as well as anybody: statue by statue, fresco by fresco, painting by painting, he painstakingly restored the artwork in these centuries-old churches, just as the Romanian people would do with their lives and their culture.

7

THE VIA FRANCIGENA, ITALY

June 2009

WE HAD TAKEN SIX OF THESE PILGRIMAGES by 2009, and although there had been some gaps in time between them, Nick and I would be in touch from time to time to discuss whether we should do another and, if so, where. We had developed a good pattern, knew how to plan and execute them, and realized, after we returned home, what a valuable experience each had been. So at some point during the winter, the thought arose of going to some of the places where St. Augustine had been, and to make him the centerpiece of the trip. Nick knew much more about his life and writings than I did, but I was familiar enough with his writings and philosophy, and as a fairly newly minted Catholic thought that such a trip would be a good incentive to read more—which I did, through the spring of 2009. Additionally, Algeria and Tunisia, in Northern Africa, were part of the world that I had never visited, they were relatively peaceful places in 2009 and we were led to believe that we would have no trouble travelling to them.

So we planned to meet in Milan, where Augustine had spent a couple of years early in his life, and then follow his path south across Italy, cross the Mediterranean to Carthage and Tunisia, where he was born, then on to Hippo in what is now Algeria where he was named Bishop in 395 and where he spent the rest of his life. Our plan was to read and discuss *The City of God*, one of his greatest works as we travelled. In preparation for this educational journey, I had read much of his *Confessions* and several books and articles about his life, his writings, and his contribution to Christianity, including Malcolm Muggeridge's *A Third Testament* and Norman Cantor's *Antiquity*.

But our plans were shelved by the Algerian Embassy in Washington. I had submitted my passport to the Embassy weeks before departure but had heard nothing. Eventually, two days before I was to leave for Europe, I was summoned to the Embassy, where I was placed in a waiting room for three or four hours, eventually to be told that I could not get a visa. Despite my most insistent prying, no reason was given, and my passport was returned. I later learned that the sleuths at the Embassy had found an article I had once written that included some pro-Israel words—enough for the Embassy to conclude that I was a threat to Algeria.

So Nick and I met in Milan and over a very long reunion dinner—and too much wine—we reminisced about past trips and much else and, of course, discussed where we would venture off to the next morning instead. There were various options—Northern Italy offered wonderful trails and many churches, monasteries, shrines, and cathedrals. Or we could venture down the Mediterranean coast and on to Sardinia and Corsica, places with much Christian history in their own right. We decided to sleep on it and regroup in the morning.

I had suggested that Nick pick up a book on Italian monasteries, which he did before leaving London. It included a couple of references to the Via Francigena—the Italian end of the network of European pilgrimage trails. We looked it up on the internet on the hotel lobby computer, and sure enough, it came to life before us—the Italian version of the Camino de Santiago.

We found a bookstore nearby and broached the subject with a clerk who, unlike American bookstore employees who know virtually nothing about what they are selling, knew the literature and the surroundings and made some great recommendations, including walking the medieval pilgrim trail to Rome. He produced a guidebook which, he explained, would get us from point to point, complete with trail descriptions, distances, places to stay and so on. The trouble was, however, that the book was in Italian, and beyond a few pasta dishes and musical terms neither of us knew a word of the language. We bought it anyway. At least it wasn't in Polish or Hungarian.

We walked for miles through Milan looking, to no avail, for signs of Augustine's time there and were surprised to find virtually nothing about him, which seemed strange since he must be one of Milan's most famous sons. Augustine received Christian instruction in Milan and was baptized there by St. Ambrose, before becoming one of the most influential Christian writers and philosophers in the history of Christendom.

Large cities never did much for our pilgrimages, so we caught a train to Piacenza, about an hour away in the heart of Emilia-Romagna, and soon found ourselves sitting in a Mass in the Basilica of St. Antonio. We then proceeded down the main road into the center—a very long, hot and tiring walk which passed no inns or hotels. After an hour or so, finding nothing, I suggested to Nick that I would inquire of my friend St. Frances Cabrini, the first American citizen to be canonized a saint (and who was born not far from Milan), who is the patroness of finding places for wayward people to stay. Nick said he vaguely knew who she was but what, he asked, did I know about her and how did I know it? I told him that I was going to dinner one evening in Washington with Michael Novak, the great Catholic theologian and writer, and several others. Michael also happened to be my Godfather when I had been received into the Catholic Church several years earlier and was a good friend. Michael had insisted on driving to the restaurant several blocks away from where we had congregated, while the rest of us walked. As he left, I told him he would never find a place to park near the restaurant. But just as we arrived on foot and he in the car, a car, parked just in front of the restaurant, pulled out of a parking spot and Michael pulled in. When I asked Michael how he had arranged such a feat, he explained that Mother Frances Cabrini had done it. "Just ask her the next time you need a place to park," Michael said, "and a place will open up." I subsequently tried it several times, almost always successfully. So I said a quick prayer to Mother Cabrini and around the next corner what should pop up but Hotel di Roma. Nick, who always took a bit of a dim view of Catholics, was quite amazed.

We spent the next morning wandering in and out of countless churches, a cathedral, and monasteries, and reading about the history of this fascinating little place, far off the beaten path. Settled by the Romans in the second century BC, it was captured and recaptured countless times by the Franks, the Lombards among others, and most recently by Napoleon. In the late eleventh century the First Crusade was proclaimed here, and the city became a trade center.

The Via Francigena was the principal road from the Holy Roman Empire to Rome. It is part of the pilgrim's network stretching 1900 kilometers from Canterbury, through England, France, and Switzerland, and into Italy and along the western side to Rome; it is one of the three great pilgrimage routes with the Camino de Santiago and the trails to Jerusalem. Starting in about the eleventh century, pilgrims began walking along the route; throughout the Middle Ages, hundreds of thousands a year travelled the pilgrimage roads on their way to the Holy City. In 2009, the Via Francigena had none of the worldwide recognition accorded to the Camino, although in subsequent years it has started gaining many more walkers. Unlike the Roman roads we think of today, it was not one route, paved and still in good shape, but several roads running more or less parallel. The routes would change depending on weather, obstacles, wars, and other dangers. The route connected abbeys rather than cities, as a Roman road or medieval trade route would, and it still connects small towns rather than the large cities. But after all, as we all know, all roads lead to Rome.

After an afternoon in Cremona and a visit to the art gallery and the violin museum, both of which housed many Strads, Guarneris, and a 1615 Amati viola (I decided I wanted it), we went on to Fidenza and the Via Francigena. We found rooms above what was billed as an "Authentic Irish Bar" which was only authentic in the noise that was coming up the stairs from the bar.

The next morning we had little trouble finding the Francigena, which was well marked and became a well-worn path as we ascended a steep hill that opened up on high plains, a mixture of farms and woods with mountains in the background. We walked to Costamezzana, and as we entered the town Mass was just starting in the fifteenth century church, a white stucco structure in as well-preserved a state as imaginable. I went in and sat in the back—few seats were empty, and in fact it appeared that the whole town must have been in the church on this clear Sunday morning in June. The whole town—and me. It looked to me, at least, that everybody else there was a local.

But nobody paid much attention to this American pilgrim, even as I walked up the aisle to take communion with the rest of them. Although the Italians, like the rest of Western Europe, are earning the reputation of turning ever more secular, Catholicism is still alive and well in the villages and small towns, at least in this part of Northern Italy.

We walked on through more picturesque towns, eventually finding a hotel in Fornova which had, of all things, a swimming pool. After about 35 kilometers, up and down hills, nothing much could have felt better. Probably few of the hundreds of thousands of medieval pilgrims who had walked from Canterbury or Northern France or elsewhere in Europe toward Rome had had the luxury of a swimming pool—but not enough guilt emerged to keep either Nick or me out of that pool.

Unlike the Camino in Spain, very few other people were on the Francigena. We would often go for half a day without seeing anybody other than an occasional farmer and people in the villages, although the locals we did meet were enormously friendly and helpful. But like the Camino the trail would vary from a grassy path through fields to rocky trails up and down mountains, then along a busy highway or along a railroad. Some were obviously the very trails from the middle ages, often worn in the earth from millions of feet over hundreds of years.

With the Apennine mountains in the background, high meadows and mixed clumps of trees before us, an occasional village or villa scattered here and there, what we saw was close to the most picturesque countryside in Italy. We passed through Burdone and eventually came to Berceto, still in Emilia-Romagna, a charming little place. We had followed a mountain trail downhill for several kilometers, suddenly entering into town and down along a narrow street with stone buildings on either side. As we walked into town we asked about hotels or hostels, but if the townspeople knew where one was apparently they were not going to tell us—until one kindly man pointed to a house with a small restaurant attached and told us to see Maria who would fix us up.

Maria, a rotund woman in her sixties who looked the part of the quintessential Italian mama, practically threw her arms around each of us and assured us that she could accommodate us. Would we like the bridal suite? She asked. We were not sure if she thought we were a gay couple—an unlikely idea, but we were able to dissuade her from that. Two rooms, please. So we followed her up three flights of stairs into simple but clean and nicely appointed little rooms. My window was wide open, and I could see back into the hills we had just left. Have a shower, she told us, and she would be waiting for us in the dining room.

This was very much a family establishment. Maria's sons, both in their thirties, a couple of grandchildren, a daughter, and who knows who else all came to the table—there were only four or five in the place, and a couple more outside—and welcomed this Englishman and American to their restaurant. A cold bottle of local white wine appeared, then some fresh bread, a bottle of olive oil, a fresh salad, and then pasta, pork, sauces and the rest.

Had it been an ordinary lazy day, the food would have been as good as what one would get in any of the best Italian restaurants in the U.S. But after thirty-six kilometers through the foothills of the Apennines, up and down, the food was nothing short of fantastic. So to bed and with a full stomach and plenty of wine it took about a minute before I was dead to the world.

In *The Path to Rome* the great French-turned-Brit Catholic writer Hillarie Belloc recounts a pilgrimage he made very early in the twentieth century, starting in Toul in Lorraine in France, through the Mosel valley, southwest across Germany and Switzerland, the length of the Ticino valley, across the Lombard plain, the Emilian way, and on to Rome. The Francigena was then impossible to find, having been out of fashion for a couple of hundred years. But having followed a straight line from Milan to Rome, and then wending his way, all on foot, through villages and over hills and through valleys, he approximated the Francigena and our route, and describes walking through many of the same little towns we found on our journey. After two World Wars and the turmoil brought to Europe by fascism and communism, reading Belloc reveals how different the world was then, but also how unchanged are so many of the things and places he records.

Fully rested the next morning, we wandered through the town and into the cathedral, which was built in the twelfth century and rebuilt in the sixteenth, plain but with wonderful stained glass windows, and looking like it had suited the citizens of Berceto well for over 900 years. An elderly priest, with white hair cut short, wire rims and a friendly smile, showed us through the church; with his limited English, probably used once a year at the outside, he explained the architecture, the statues, the windows, and so on.

The road out of Berceto was paved but not busy. Soon it became quite steep and seemed to go on and on, eventually to the top of a mountain where there were little cafes and a gift shop selling snacks and cold drinks. As we walked up the mountain we were passed by about sixty bicycles, all ridden by sixty-to-seventy-year-old, skinny-butted men decked out in the most expensive Spandex outfits, biking shoes, and little hats, their legs bulging muscles. Everything about them looked like they had just stepped out of the high fashion edition of the periodico sportivo of Northern Italy. When we arrived at the top, a bit desheveled, probably unshaven, and carrying our old packsacks, I overheard one of these guys disdainfully mutter to his friend, "Pelligirini, pelligrini..." ("Pilgrims, pilgrims...").

From there the route was supposed to take us to Pontromoli, but we took a wrong turn somewhere—the Francigena is well marked in some spots, but marked not at all in others—and walked through vineyards, orchards, fields, and tiny villages clinging to high cliffs. We forded a number of streams, up and down steep mountainsides and eventually, exhausted, got back on to the road to Pontraomoli, crossing from Emilio-Romagna into Tuscany.

The paths were steep, sometimes difficult to find, but walking on the roads with cars and trucks passing within a foot of us was worse. There was no question it was a strenuous exercise, made more so by a twenty-five pound backpack. The walking would almost become second-nature, a mind-set, just a matter of getting to the next place. Pain was a constant, whether it was a blister, sore muscle, shin splint, or joint somewhere that told me it was overused. But the pain became an afterthought, mere background noise, particularly when the plight of the medieval pilgrims popped into mind. Their pain had no Motrin, their blisters no Neosporin or Dr. Scholls plasters, their feet no high-tech boots, and their appetites no luscious, hot Italian meal with a bottle of red wine waiting at the end of the day followed by a warm bed with clean sheets to fall into. Ours was not an authentic medieval pilgrimage, not by a long shot, but it was still a pilgrimage in the modern Christian world, and what we were doing was more rewarding because of the agony, such as it was, that we were putting ourselves through.

Once again, as we arrived in Pontremoli there was no obvious hotel or hostel. What a difference from Germany, Switzerland, and Austria, where every little village has at least two pensions or Gasthäuser. But a friendly gent directed us to what looked like an ordinary house and told us to ask for Francesca, who indeed ran a little B&B which proved to be very comfortable and most welcome to our feet and legs—we had covered about 35 kilometers.

Francesca was a well-fed, plump little soul who seemed at peace with the world, and turned out to be the perfect hostess and tour guide. After breakfast she offered to show us this classic Italian medieval village, undiscovered by tourists. First stop was the Duomo, situated in the center of the old town and surrounded by a bustling market square. Construction of the Duomo started in 1636, in the peak of the Baroque. This church was covered with stuccos, statues of angels and saints, and all the trappings of a Baroque church. Much of the old city wall was still intact, complete with a tower near the Duomo, which Francesca proudly told us was built in 1332 to keep rival families apart from each other but had been transformed into a clock tower in the mid-1500s.

From Pontremoli we made our way to Lucca, partially on foot, partially by train which, after plodding along on foot for a few days, was incredibly luxurious, comfortable and fast. It is surprising how quickly, while walking for miles at a time, imagining what pilgrims 500 years ago went through, one forgets what modern life is like, and how surprising it feels to be on a train, whisking along at sixty miles per hour, covering in a few minutes what might take hours on foot.

Lucca, which I had visited once years earlier, is a fabulous medieval city completely surrounded by an eleventh century wall wide enough to drive cars on the top. And in fact, as a local fellow we bumped into explained, the wall had been used as an automobile race track—something only an Italian could think of doing. The races went on for a year or so before more sober bureaucrats found it to be an unseemly practice and stopped it; today the wall encompassing the city is a quiet and sedate walking and bicycle path.

Lucca is a well-preserved provincial capital city, founded about 150 BC, which played an important role in Roman times—Julius Caesar established his first triumvirate there—and into the Middle Ages, when it became Italy's most important silk trading post. Dante spent much of his later life in exile in Lucca, and it was home to countless wealthy Roman families who dominated life there well into modern times. We wandered through the narrow streets, visited church after church—there was a medieval church on virtually every corner, each more stunning than the last. We went into several, usually stopping to offer a quick prayer and to admire the architecture, the workmanship, and the sense of grace that seemed to emanate from these buildings which had seen so many generations of worshipers, of pilgrims and probably of heathens and degenerates trying to right their lives with Christ.

From Lucca we made our way, mostly on foot but intermittently by bus and train, to San Gimignano, a classic unspoiled medieval city perched on top of a hill and famous for its towers, each built by a family trying to outdo its neighbors' tower, all still standing after seven or eight hundred years and all in as good shape as they were when built. Surrounded by an intact wall, San Gemignano has numerous Romanesque and Gothic churches, often squeezed between provincial government buildings, counting houses, palatial family compounds and much more. The churches have some fine examples of Medieval frescos from the fourteenth and fifteenth centuries.

Saint Augustine spent several weeks in San Gimignano on his way from Milan to Rome. The second largest church in town, Sant'Agostino, is named for him and is a center of Augustinian culture and spirituality as well as the home of a set of frescoes, commissioned in the late fifteenth century, illustrating scenes from his life. As our trip was originally designed to follow in the steps of Augustine, aborted when the Algerians refused to give me a visa, San Gimignano provided a forum for further discussion and observation about this fourth century saint who has had such a profound impact on the Christian faith. I had brought along a copy of a collection of Augustine's *Confessions* and other writings which was still in my backpack, so we found a bench on the square in front of Sant'Agostino and turned to a random page, which happened to be from Confession XI on the creation of the world. Augustine says that the creation of human beings continues throughout life; that we live through dark and turbulent troubles as well as good times. But it is all intended, he says, to enlighten us about God and empowers us on our journey of faith. It is creative grace, he wrote, that brings us to be "perfected, illumined and beatified." We agreed that this trip was certainly a long way from being part of the dark and turbulent, but instead one that strengthened our faith. Mine, anyway.

The Towers of San Gemignano, Italy

The Sant'Agostino church, finished in 1298, is constructed around a single-aisle with three side chapels and an open-roof truss. It is a typical example of Gothic church architecture found in central Italy. Typical, that is, but for the frescoes, which were added some two hundred years after the church was finished; they include seventeen scenes from Saint Augustine's life and have been interpreted as a painted metaphor of striving to reach God. Evil, according to Augustine, comes from our own desires rather than from external influences. Certainly there is a devil to urge us on to our own desires, but damnation is the result of what goes on inside of each of us, and salvation is God's gift to us—what we call God's grace.

We left San Gimignano before six the next morning, walking through small villages, gravel roads, and narrow paths, eventually making our way to Monteriggioni, another village perched on top of a hill. Compared to San Gimignano, Monteriggioni was a study in simplicity. It had not become a tourist destination; the square in the center of town, rather than full of vendors selling postcards and trinkets was virtually empty, and the people, rather than foreign tourists, appeared to be locals. We found an outdoor café and had a coffee and pastry before moving on. The town is surrounded by a circular wall more than 500 meters in length, built in the thirteenth century to protect the city from invading armies—of which there were many over the next several hundred years. The wall has fourteen towers set at equal distances, and two gates. One, the Porta Fiorentina, opens toward Florence to the north, and the other, the Porta Romana, faces Rome to the south. The main piazza, the Piazza Roma, is dominated by a Romanesque and unadorned fourteenth-century church, which appeared not to have changed much over the ensuing 700 years. Monteriggioni gained its place in literature and history from the poet Dante Alighieri, who was inspired by the turrets there in describing the ring of giants encircling the Infernal abyss.

We walked on, spending all afternoon on delightful narrow trails and roads through fields and forests—trails that seemed unchanged from when pilgrims crossed them 500 years earlier.

Late in the afternoon, walking on a narrow country road, we passed an elderly man cutting weeds near the gate to his house. After brief greetings, we asked if we could get some water from him and he asked us to come into his yard, where we sat down around a little table in a shady corner. His English was as bad as our Italian, but somehow we managed to strike up a conversation. Water was obviously not enough to satisfy his hospitality, and a plate of fresh fruit emerged, all from the trees in his yard, followed by some pastries and eventually a bottle of wine made, he proudly told us, by him from his own grapes. After an hour or so we pushed along, up and down along a paved road on the way to Siena, where we arrived, very tired and with very sore feet, just as darkness enveloped the city.

Since this trip was a last minute decision, we did not have a terminus, so we had no idea where we would wind up. But both Nick and I had plane tickets from Rome, so Siena turned out to be the last stop. We vowed that we would come back another time and finish walking to Rome. I had read somewhere that this sort of walking, carrying a 25-pound pack, constantly going up and down and maintaining a fast pace, burned about 600 calories an hour. As we arrived in Siena, thirty-three kilometers further toward Rome than where we had started the day, our stomachs told us that we had indeed burned up enough energy to warrant a good dinner. I have always allowed that it is nearly impossible to get a bad meal in Italy, and certainly the food was one of the highlights of this trip. If Italian meals are always tasty, try them after a long day on foot, constantly walking up and down hills and burning 600 calories an hour.

I caught an early morning train to Rome, but being Italian it was an hour or so late arriving there and I missed the plane, which necessitated spending an extra day, a Sunday, wandering through the Eternal City. I must have gone into at least a dozen different churches, including Mass at St. Peters. Although I had cursed the late Italian train earlier, by the end of the day, I said a prayer of thanks that I had an extra day, without need to be anywhere in particular, in Rome.

The Via Francigena is an open-air history museum, available to anybody who wants to look with no admission fee. Every mile produces evidence of the crusades, of a king or prince, or more likely the tens of thousands of peasants and common people on their way to Rome. Near Buceto, crossing a stone bridge, we saw a plaque commemorating the fact that Napoleon had crossed it. And speaking of bridges, we crossed everything from grand Roman arched ones to narrow medieval ones wide enough for a horse and small buggy, all still used as if they had been built yesterday, the masonry perfectly designed, the stones fitting perfectly together and still serving the purpose for which they were built.

Walking on the Via Francigena was anything but idle, mindless travel. Every mile offered another piece of history, from the churches, the bridges, the castles, the road itself. Walking became a mindset—we pressed along, one step at a time. Shin pain, ankle pain, knee pain, blisters, stiff muscles became second nature and were tucked away in the back of our minds. Whether we walked on steep, narrow paths, along busy highways, or through pastoral ancient roads through the woods, whether we walked silently admiring the scenery, reflecting on the last historical marvel, or deep in conversation, we maintained our sense of purpose for doing this at all.

From a spiritual perspective, the Via Francigena is overwhelming. The power of Christianity is everywhere, and particularly the power of the Catholic Church. Nick and I had walked the Camino before I had become a Catholic—which had, in the end, probably been one of the things that convinced me to convert. But now, as a new Catholic, the thought of those millions of people from all walks of life—from paupers and criminals to noblemen and priests—walking from Northern Europe to Rome in honor of the Savior Jesus Christ, seemed to me to embody the universality of Catholicism and the dedication it engendered among its people.

Two of the things that had attracted me to Catholicism were, first, the history and the reach of the Church. Christianity, and particularly Catholicism, defined Western civilization. It had gone hand in hand with the history of Europe, had established the foundation of art, music, architecture and the rest of the culture. It was everywhere, in every place and in virtually every heart and soul. What we saw on the Via Francigena was the Catholic Church, in one form or another, over and over, day after day. It made me very happy that I was part of it, and that it was now part of me. In Italy in the Middle Ages, as in most of Europe, the Church was a part of everything, and every life was lived to serve the Church.

Second was the fact that the Church is the body of Jesus Christ—something that was entirely missing in Protestantism. Pilgrims walked hundreds of miles to Rome not to see the buildings, but to honor their Savior and all that he meant to them. I am not sure if one can really understand that without following in their footsteps.

For me, walking the Via Fancigena was one of the most satisfying of all the trips.

8

ALBANIA

June 2010

IN FEBRUARY OF 2010, Nick was in Washington, and over a long dinner together the topic of another trip came up. We had taken seven of these trips together over the past several years; they were beginning to become the norm rather than the exception, and we agreed that another was in order.

The Italian trip on the Via Fancigena had been a great success, and we tossed around several ideas over dinner, including a couple of places in Western Europe. By this point, we already had been on trips in Spain, France, Italy and Greece, plus trips to the Arab world, in Turkey and Syria. So, I suggested Albania—it was the most Muslim country in Europe, but about half of its residents were Catholics or Orthodox, so I thought it would be a unique experience to visit a place that thus combined Christianity and Islam in its population.

I was also interested in Albania as it had been the most

repressive country in the old East Bloc—a veritable North Korea—and had totally outlawed all religion and shut down all churches, mosques, and other religious sites, turning them into warehouses, stables, military barracks, or whatever else, and killed hundreds of priests, nuns, monks, imams, and other religious people. The communist leader Enver Hoxha made Romania's Nicolae Ceauşescu look like a piker. Albania had also had the most difficult time, of all the East Bloc countries, coming out of its communist past and into the free West.

And so we agreed—Albania would make a fascinating trip.

Bordering on Greece and just across the Adriatic from southern Italy, Albania is the poorest country in Europe, about the size of Maryland but with 7000-foot mountains. It had a long history of lawlessness, and after communism fell, was among other things the stolen car capital of the world. Its tumultuous history, both before the twentieth century and during it, tells one something of the sort of place it later became.

Albania was part of the Roman Empire until it was conquered by the Slavs, later by the Bulgarians, and ultimately by the Ottoman Empire. The Turks kicked it around for centuries until the First Balkan War in 1912, and with the dissolution of Turkish rule, Albanians found their country invaded by Serbs, Bulgarians, and Greeks, all of whom wanted pieces of it, until a truce in 1913, supervised by the Great Powers, created an independent country. But that only lasted for a year or so when the Serbs again invaded, followed closely by troops from the Hapsburg's Austro-Hungarian Empire, who were actually welcomed, in pursuit of the Serbs. By the end of World War I and the demise of Austria-Hungary, Albania was again thrown into turmoil, and in 1939 Mussolini's forces invaded, soon followed by the Greeks bent on defeating the Italians. The collapse of Mussolini's regime in 1943 brought in the Germans, and in 1945 the place descended into hell with the emergence of Enver Hoxha, a young resistance fighter turned communist who eventually became head of state. The role model of Kim Jong Il, Hoxha is described by Albanians as "Stalin on steroids."

Albania started its journey into communism as part of Yugoslavia, but broke that off in 1948 because Hoxha found Tito too moderate. He then signed up with Stalin, who had about the right temperament, but that love affair soured after Stalin died in 1953 and Khrushchev turned out to be a squish, so Hoxha partnered with communist China instead, which lasted until 1978 when he decided Mao was a middle-of-the-roader and threw him out and decided to go it alone, friendless, at least outside of American Ivy League faculty lounges. In the meantime Hoxha turned the country into a police state to end all police states, armed it to the teeth, built 150,000 mushroom-looking concrete bunkers to repel western infiltrators, declared the country an atheist state—the only country in the history of the world ever to be so designated—and put together an internal security apparatus that made the East German Stasi look like child's play. He locked the place down, eliminating almost all contact with the outside world, maintaining diplomatic relations with only a few Warsaw Pact countries that met the test of severity.

With the fall of communism in the early nineties, Albania had the most difficult time of any East-bloc country returning to freedom, and only after ten years of lawlessness, riots, organized street crime, suppression, attempts by thousands to flee to Greece and Italy, and a pyramid scheme that practically cleaned out the country, did it begin to achieve a degree of normality and begin to join the civilized world.

Nick and I thought it would be fascinating to learn what happened when such a tyrannical place achieves liberty. What transpires when those in a designated atheistic state are allowed again to practice their faith and to worship? What are the consequences when every scintilla of entrepreneurial spirit has been crushed and then people are again permitted to make a living as they see fit? What happens in a situation where the state controlled absolutely every shred of human endeavor, and then returned to a relatively benign and democratic entity? We thought we would try to find out. And so the unusual destination for our eighth pilgrimage together was chosen—with a different sort of spiritual goal than our previous pilgrimages.

Cold War Bunker, Albania

We met in Tirana and proceeded, over the next ten days, to cover much of Albania, travelling in a variety of ways: walking for full days at a time, travelling in mini-buses and a rowboat, hitchhiking and, for part of the trip, riding in a chauffeur-driven Mercedes. We stayed in upscale and $10-a-night hotels, inns, and a farmhouse, and we talked to dozens upon dozens of every sort of person.

I arrived from Rome at Tirana's Mother Teresa Airport—named for the recently sainted Albanian nun who is now considered a national hero. Imagine what the ACLU would do if an airport in the U.S. were named for a nun—have a heyday in court while secular liberalism cried out in agony. But this was quite a switch for a place like Albania. The Albanian Constitution of 1976 unabashedly declared, "The State recognizes no religion, and supports and carries out atheistic propaganda in order to implant a scientific materialistic world outlook in people." The state not only banned religion but also shot priests, nuns, monks, and Muslim clerics. It bulldozed churches or, if they were old enough, turned them into warehouses and stables after painting out every fresco, painting and vestige of religious adornment, and imprisoned anybody who even breathed a word about any sort of religion.

My plane arrived after midnight, and as I landed I hoped a taxi would be available to take me into town. I was relieved when a bevy of cab drivers were waiting as I claimed my luggage. I wondered if in fact these guys were really cab drivers or muggers, and was surprised when mine ushered me into a new and very clean Mercedes. I looked around as we drove into Tirana, and it seemed that every car on the road was also either a new Mercedes or BMW. Where, I wondered, did this poor country happen on all these expensive cars?

Nick had gone to bed by the time I arrived, so we met for breakfast in the hotel the next morning, where we caught up and examined our guidebooks and maps. Nick had made arrangements to meet up with an old friend who was now living in Tirana and was married to an Albanian, so we went to their walk-up apartment in what looked like a pre-war building.

"Sorry for the tight space," she said as we entered. "The place is spacious by Tirana standards, but a far cry from what most American families with two children have." Her husband, who was travelling, worked for an international Christian NGO, she told us, working mostly on poverty issues. She had been in Albania for almost two years, had travelled around the country with her husband, and had a good grasp of culture, politics, and the economic situation. "As an American, I am astounded by how poor Albania still is," she told us.

"If Albania is so poor," I asked her, "where do all these expensive German cars come from?" She broke out laughing. "Stolen. Albania is the car theft capital of the world," she told us. "Gangs travel to Western Europe, steal the cars, and drive them back here and sell them." She told us that a survey of BMW X5s (the four-wheel drive luxury SUV) situated in Tirana found 118 of them, and all but ten had identical vehicle identification numbers. She said that it was no secret that Albania had the reputation of being the most lawless country in Europe. "We like to think it is getting over it," she said. Albania was trying to get into both NATO and the European Union, she said, but thought it would be a long time before that happened. "The EU has told Albania that it has to get control of the rule of law before it will even be considered," she said.

Nick asked her about the state of religion in the country. "As interesting as any place in the world," she said. After the fall of communism there was an influx of Catholic, Evangelical,

Orthodox Christian, and Muslim missionaries, prepared to try to undo what the atheistic communist government had done. "Hundreds of thousands of Bibles and copies of the Koran have been distributed," she said. "Foreign groups have rebuilt churches and mosques and done so much else to try to reinstitute religious life," she explained. Some have worked, she said, and many have gone home disappointed. Although things were far different than during the communist times, much remained to be done.

"As you travel through the country, you will see many churches, mosques, and other religious buildings," she said. "Stop whenever you can, engage whomever you meet in conversation about religion. You will be surprised what you hear."

After a couple of hours of enlightening conversation, we walked a few blocks to one of the few modern high-rise buildings in Tirana and were whisked to the top floor in a New York–style elevator, where we were escorted to a table overlooking the city and mountains in the distance. As we approached the table, a tall and well-dressed man in his early forties rose and greeted us. "Alex Nushi," he said. A friend of Nick's in Frankfurt had suggested that we meet with him. A most gracious man, Nushi was the chief legal officer at one of the large Albanian banks, a sophisticated, well-educated fellow, and a dedicated Christian. He had somehow weathered the communist years and was well-informed, needless to say, about all things Albanian. We talked about the current political situation, the economic struggles in which the country was still engaged, and the political and economic history of the country since 1989. It was a fairly grim picture, but Alex offered a ray of optimism that things were finally beginning to come together.

"You seem fairly optimistic about life here," Nick said.

"Why's that?" Alex explained that his Christianity was the root of his sense of well-being, even in the direst circumstances. "After what this country went through during the communist time, having the freedom to say what we want to say, the religious freedom that we now have, is such a transformation that it is mind-boggling," he said.

I asked him about the state of the Christian church here, whether the people have firm beliefs, and particularly where the beliefs come from, given the enforced atheism that was the law for so long. He responded that the repression dictated by communism had endured for over forty years, meaning that it was multi-generational. "People would be imprisoned for years for even having a Bible in their house. Everybody was encouraged to report everybody else, even children against their parents. It was part of the communist mindset, establishing a culture where nobody trusted anybody else," he said. Because children were prohibited from learning anything about religion, the entire younger generations knew nothing about it, he explained. They didn't only distrust religious figures and their message, as was the case in the Soviet Union. Many people were simply totally ignorant about it. "Overcoming that," he said, "is very difficult."

Over an elegantly served lunch, Alex explained that Western churches, in addition to sending missionaries, had sent adequate amounts of money with which to rebuild and refurbish churches. He urged us to stop wherever we saw old churches as we travelled across the country. "Hoxha destroyed newer churches, but he thought that the older ones reflected the history of our country, so rather than raze them, he stripped the interiors but left the buildings. Many of those are now being rebuilt." Churches built in the eleventh and twelfth centuries and even a few from the second century remained, he told us. Because many religious organizations, particularly the Catholic and Orthodox churches, had sent missionaries, artisans, and money to help rebuild and restore churches and re-establish organized religion, nearly 1500 churches had been built or restored since the fall of communism. Nushi said he was convinced that as opportunities for religious education improved, the hunger for spiritual fulfillment would overcome ignorance, and that faith would return.

I commented that compared to secular Western Europe, religion could be thriving within the next couple of decades in Albania.

"By no means do I imply that there is no religious life in our country," he said. "There is a church on a mountaintop not far from Tirana where pilgrims go every June by the hundreds of thousands—Protestants, Catholics, Orthodox, Muslims, even atheists. It will happen next week," he told us. "You need to go there to see it."

The religious population in modern Albania is a mix of Christians and Muslims. Of those who have returned to faith, it is estimated that half are Muslims, 30 percent Orthodox, and 20 percent Catholic, with a smattering of Evangelicals, although much of the population continues to be atheist. The Muslims are known as Bektashi, a mystic sect that is unique to the Balkans; Albania's Bektashis are moderate and peaceful people, get along well with Christians (and in fact intermarry and convert to Christianity without objection), but are considered infidels by the Wahabis. Over the course of our journey, we visited many mosques that had been reopened or rebuilt, as well as Christian churches and monasteries, and we even found a new Orthodox monastery being built from the ground up.

The infrastructure was a different story. No Russian-built subway systems were constructed here, as in Warsaw and Budapest—just dusty, pot-hole laden, overcrowded roads, often blocked with herds of sheep and goats, people riding on donkeys, and flocks of chickens forcing those shiny Mercedes onto the shoulder. The country is about the size of Maryland, and the only airport is Mother Teresa Airport in the capital; what railroads exist are falling apart and used only for freight, leaving the primary means of transportation to an improvised system of entrepreneur-owned buses and minivans (also mostly Mercedes).

Nick had arranged for a car and driver to take us around for the first three or four days; the driver, Simon Arapi, met us later in the day in his well-cared for Mercedes (he later explained that it was the only car that could survive hundreds of thousands of miles on Albanian roads). Simon had been referred to Nick by a friend in London who had spent some time in Tirana several years earlier; Simon had driven for the British Embassy for several years, spoke English well, and knew Albania like the palm of his hand. He had travelled down virtually every road in the country, knew everything about everywhere we went, seemed to know somebody in every town, and was a delightful travelling companion.

We drove out of Tirana to Durresi, not far northwest of Tirana, located on a beautiful bay, an important Adriatic port since the seventh century BC. It became one of the European starting points of the Via Egnatia, the Roman road built in the second century BC that connected Europe and Byzantium and which we would travel on in Macedonia and Greece in 2017. The Via Egnatia made Durresi an important Roman outpost. We walked up to the amphitheater, which could accommodate some 15,000 people—the largest in the Balkans and built in the second century. "After it was abandoned by the Romans in about the fifth century, it was taken over by Christians who decorated the walls of the vaults underneath with mosaics of the saints and angels," Simon told us. The mosaics were still visible.

Simon pointed us to King Zog's abandoned and ransacked pink palace, built on a hilltop in the 1930s by one of the most bizarre political figures of the twentieth century. "He was a self-appointed dictator and king who ruled Albania from 1928 until the country was seized by the Italians in 1939," Simon explained. Signs told us that the palace was permanently closed (thieves had broken in several years earlier and stolen everything of value) and surrounded by barbed wire. We walked up the hill and were able to squeeze through gaps in the fence, and enjoyed a self-guided tour of this outlandish spot, which offered fabulous views of the city and the Adriatic.

A most moving stop was a visit to a small Catholic church in Durresi where eight priests, monks, and nuns were shot, inside the church, by the Hoxha regime as part of its efforts to cleanse the country of anything religious. A priest showed us around the church and a wall of pictures of the martyrs, adorned with flowers. "Hoxha saw Jesus Christ as a threat to him," the priest told us in rather broken English. "To rule the way he did, he thought he needed the total dedication of the people, without competition from God." He told us that Catholics, Orthodox Christians, and Muslims were all treated the same—most clerics were killed, and a few were lucky enough to spend years in prison doing hard labor (in 2016, Pope Francis named to the College of Cardinals one of those priests who had spent twenty-eight years in communist labor camps). Pope Francis also beatified thirty-eight murdered Albanian priests in 2016, including those from Durresi. The scene stayed in the forefront of my mind for weeks.

Simon, who was a Christian, confirmed Alex's earlier opinion that Christianity might have been suppressed during the communist era, but that it did not die. "Let me show you how it thrives in Albania," he said, and drove us to a small Catholic church perched high on a mountainside under a huge white cross, probably about 80 to 100 feet high, visible from twenty miles away. This was the place Alex had recommended that we see.

Known as the Church of Laci, it was built in the twelfth century and dedicated to St. Anthony of Padua. Near the church, which is built into the hillside, is a huge outdoor altar. A young Albanian priest approached us, and Simon translated for us. The next week, the priest told us, the church would host a pilgrimage of Christians who would walk about five miles from the valley, along a steep, hot, and winding road, and vertically up about 2000 feet to spend the day in prayer. "How many people do you expect?" I asked him. "Last year we had about 250,000," he responded. "We expect about twice that many this year." And, in fact, it is estimated that about half a million people walked up the mountain—not bad, in a population of fewer than four million people—people who would have gone to prison until twenty years ago if they even mentioned religion.

We drove on through incredible mountain roads—narrow, steep with many curves, sometimes paved, sometimes gravel. To get to any place from any other it was necessary to go over the top of a 7000-foot mountain. Although it looked a bit like the Appalachians, there were no gaps between the mountains, so the only path was over them. So if you were going from one city to another 30 miles as the crow flies, the actual distance might be 100 miles at 30 mph all the way.

Simon dropped us off at his cousin's farm, which doubled as a restaurant and sort of B&B, situated on the shore of a large lake. The plan was to meet Simon again in three days; in the meantime we would fend for ourselves, taking public transportation, such as public transportation in Albania is. The restaurant part of the establishment was an outdoor porch; we were the only guests, but the grilled meat and fresh vegetables were tasty and well prepared. The accommodations were something else again. The bathroom had gone through some sort of crisis and did not work. The toilet was a bucket and a hose to wash things away. The beds were army cots without sheets. But we took it all in stride with plenty of laughs and made it through the night.

The couple that ran the place had a very amusing son, probably twelve or so, who was the original extrovert and who knew just enough English to get along and keep us entertained. At breakfast the boy offered to row us across the lake for a small fee, so that we could avoid a long walk to the next town. Not more than a hundred yards from the dock the boy lit up a cigarette, explaining that this was forbidden at home, but presumably being on the water, the parents were out of sight and it was, therefore, allowed. After an hour or so, he dropped us on the other side and we proceeded along a dusty road of sorts, which the map indicated would get us to Perlat, where we could catch a bus to Berati, a rather major location.

We must have taken a wrong turn, as we walked for a couple of hours and seemed to be getting nowhere. No markers, directions, or signs indicated that we were making headway, at least until we came to a farm road, leading to a house and barn a couple of hundred yards from the road. As we approached the owner, a smiley peasant appeared. Here was another situation, which we had encountered so often, where there was not a common word between us but we were nevertheless able to get the point across—that being, could the man drive us into town for a fee? Indeed he would, but he had a situation he needed to attend to and would be with us shortly. In ten minutes or so he emerged, a great smile on his face and covered, from head to toe, with blood—and holding a severed pig's head which he proudly presented to us with a good-natured laugh. He disappeared, only to return in a few minutes all cleaned up with fresh clothes and bottles of cold water and snacks and proceeded to drive us the 20 kilometers or so into Berati.

First settled in at least 2000 BC, Berati is one of the oldest cities in Albania, and after so many years still retains its charm. We walked up to the citadel at the top of a hill on the edge of the city. In the citadel compound we walked past several large houses, several medieval churches and a couple of the oldest mosques in Albania, as well as the best antiquities museum in the Balkans; its historical significance apparently saved it from Enver Hoxha's anti-religious wrath.

From there, we faced several days of public transportation. Albania has no railroads; it is too small for domestic air travel, and there are no organized bus routes. Instead, the central square is a sort of "slug line;" mini vans and small buses wait, with a destination sign in the window, and when they are full, off they go. The fare is the equivalent of a dollar or two. Over the mountains, on twisty and dusty roads, often hair-raising s-curves without any barriers, and a thousand foot drop just a foot or two from the wheel of the bus, through astounding scenery, any trip is often four to five hours long with a rest stop along the way. Quite efficient, these little inexpensive buses are probably the best way to get a sense of the place and to make new friends along the way, at least if you can make friends where no word between the two of you can be understood.

We caught a minibus at the town square going to Gjirokaster, perhaps 75 kilometers as the crow flies, but a three-hour trip over two mountain passes along narrow, windy roads. Nick and I were the only non-Albanians in the bus, and nobody seemed to speak anything but their native tongue but from the laughter we assumed we were the butt of many jokes. However, people were friendly, even to the point of offering chunks of chocolate and sips from their water jugs.

Gjirokaster is Enver Hoxha's hometown, no matter of pride to its current residents; except for its connection to him, it is a charming place, built along a river and between two mountains. Dating from the thirteenth century, the central part of town is now virtually automobile free; the minibus dropped us a short walk from the center. The city had been made a UNESCO World Heritage Site a couple of years earlier, largely because of its traditional nineteenth-century stone houses, all built in a similar architectural style, and cobblestone streets. After an early dinner of excellent local dishes, we walked through these streets to the top of an adjoining hill to the castle—the largest castle in Albania, the guide told us, first built in the fourth century and now a museum. The place was used as a prison during World War II by the Germans and retained during the communist period; cells are still there, including a number of torture chambers. The castle includes an armaments museum of little interest, with the exception of a two-seater U.S. Air Force jet which was allegedly forced down in 1957 and advertised as an American spy plane.

"It was not actually forced down at all," the guard told us, "but had engine trouble and made an emergency landing. Hoxha was paranoid about everything and wanted everybody else in the country to be paranoid also. So he had this plane presented as a spy plane." The guard's reaction to Hoxha was typical of the complete contempt Albanians had for the man.

The next morning we caught a minibus to Saranda, a resort city situated in the southernmost corner of the country, on the Ionian Sea, just a few miles from the Greek Island of Corfu and directly east of the heel of the Italian boot. The beach was lined with high-rise hotels; we found an inexpensive one, a converted Soviet-style apartment building—the sort that populates every communist city in the world. We concluded that no amount of renovation could make them habitable, but I was pleased, after having seen so many in so many different parts of the world, to spend one night in one.

Nick and I took a long walk along the boardwalk, Corfu in the distance, the sun going down into the Mediterranean beyond. Behind us the town itself was a maze of glitzy hotels and condominiums, lots of neon lights above shops and bars. Albanians think of it as their Riviera; Western Europeans think of it as the inexpensive alternative to the Riviera. But the Albanians were pleased to have the Euros. We concluded it could be one of a thousand similar places, all vying for the free-spending tourists anxious to soak up sun and sin.

We took a short bus ride, the following day, to Butrint, a 2500-year-old city which had recently been turned into a national park. It was a major city for both the Greeks and later the Romans. Much of the construction dates from the fourth century BC, including a large amphitheater, and featured the usual array of foundations, columns, and mosaics. A helpful guide approached us and, with reasonable English, gave us a brief history lesson. I asked him what went on here during the Hoxha regime. "Not much," he replied. "The government was too busy protecting the country from invaders and suppressing religion, the people too busy finding enough to eat to bother with this place." But after the thaw, in 1990, he told us, people began to sack the place, stealing Greek and Roman statues and other antiquities to sell. More evidence of the lawlessness so prevalent in this country, I commented to Nick. An enterprising group organized a foundation, the guide told us, apparently got Western money, and started preserving it. Ultimately, UNESCO made it a World Heritage Site.

"Soon after Constantine made Christianity the dominant religion of the Roman Empire," the guide explained, "Butrint became an episcopal center, a bishop was installed, and the Romans built a large basilica, first in the sixth century AD and rebuilt several times since, and a baptistry." He walked along stone paths and past mosaic floors, still in surprisingly good shape, to point out these monuments, both of which still stand in good state of repair. The dry and warm weather, the guide explained, was the reason these places were still in such good shape, as opposed to the damp and cold conditions found in Northern Europe.

Here, for me, was more evidence of the incredible reach of Christianity and the impact it has had on Western civilization. I mentioned to Alex that even in this remote corner of the world, Christianity thrived, and its message of hope and faith was enough to convince the powerful Romans to expend their wealth in a place such as this. What, I wondered, would this country have been without it?

From Butrint we spent much of the next day walking, first along a trail up the mountain, onto back roads and eventually to a small town where we found a little hotel. Then we spent an entire day on three different minibuses to Korçë; some of the way was along the Via Egnatia, the Roman road built before the birth of Christ which stretched from Constantinople, across Greece and to northern Albania, and which we would bicycle along in 2017. Over mountain after mountain, into deep valleys and through countless tiny villages, the scenery was picture perfect, the roads populated with peasants driving horses and mules pulling hay wagons, chickens, ducks, and geese in the road, children playing something that looked like hopscotch who would step to the side as we passed. But for the few cars and trucks, nothing much appeared to have changed over hundreds of years. However, if you looked hard, modernity was to be seen there also; we passed a peasant woman, dressed in a colorful dress and apron, a scarf around her head, riding sidesaddle on a donkey, holding a pitchfork and talking on a cell phone.

Korçë is situated high above sea level and is considered the most civilized city in Albania. Wide streets, stately houses and a pleasant city square make for an attractive place. Shortly after arriving we stopped at a bank to get some cash; the teller spoke no English, but beckoned us to wait for a few minutes to call a friend. Shortly an attractive woman appeared who introduced herself as Ana, the local English teacher. She would welcome, she said, a chance to speak with an American and a Brit, practice her English, brush up on political events and, in the process, introduce us to Korçë. What a lucky break!

Ana lived in a nearby farm village where she had grown up

and walked for about an hour each way to and from Korçë. She learned English at the university, she said, but had never been to an English-speaking country. Nevertheless, as with many Europeans, her English was first rate.

As we walked through the main square and up a side street, she talked about the city's modern history. Korçë had been occupied by the Greeks several times in the past 100 years, she said, and by the French after World War I, but ultimately returned to Albania in 1921. It had weathered the Hoxha-Communist time, she said, but suffered from the isolation from the rest of the world, the poverty, and suppression. Many of the buildings looked shabby, some in total disrepair. Ana said things were slowly being repaired, but money was always in short supply.

Her students, she said, were anxious to learn more about the U.S, which was a favorite topic of her classes and their readings. "Americans are well liked here," she said, "although we rarely see American tourists, which is why I am so pleased to be talking to you." She was anxious to know everything I could tell her about politics, cultural matters, and, of course, Obama. Many residents, she told me, had relatives in the U.S.—when the Greeks occupied the city after World War I, many Albanians immigrated to the U.S. In fact, she said, it is said that most Albanians in America came from Korçë. (After returning home I did verify that to be true; a large percentage settled in and around Boston.)

As we walked we passed a mosque under construction, and Nick asked what the religious composition of Korçë was. "We have Muslims, Catholics and Orthodox here," Ana said. "About one third of each." I asked how they got along with each other.

"Very well," she answered. "They live in the same

neighborhoods, go to the same schools, they even intermarry." I asked whether other churches were also being built. "Built new and renovated," she answered. This particular mosque was being paid for by the Albanian government. The people who attend there are mostly Bektashi, Ana said, they are peaceful people who get along well with all other religions. "The government believes that by building mosques and encouraging responsible religious practice it will keep extremism and violence out of our culture."

I asked whether religion is taught in the schools, and she said indeed it was—that all three religions were taught. The government guarantees religious freedom, she said, but takes no sides on which religion, and in fact remains secular in all respects.

After an hour or so we bid farewell to Ana. Although we had found her a font of information, it was clear that she was even more pleased to have spoken with us than we with her.

We had arranged to meet Simon in Korçë the next morning, and spend our last couple of days travelling to Elbasan, then back to Tirana. We were glad to see him and be out of the minibuses and into his Mercedes. He had arranged for us to stop at the house of one of his uncles—a charming log house built high on a hill overlooking Lake Ohrid. The uncle had invited several friends, none of whom spoke any English, but Simon acted as translator. Over a meal of grilled game, which the uncle had killed, we laughed and carried on as if we had known each other for years, everybody as friendly and warm-hearted as could be. Such an event, I commented to Nick, is the sort of thing most tourists never see, but which reaffirms the natural friendship that exists among all people, whoever they are and wherever they may be.

Back in Tirana, we went to an old school which had been turned into a retreat center by American Evangelicals—a friend in Washington had suggested we look them up. The center was populated by several college-age American students who passed out Bibles on the streets and would talk to willing Albanians, doing their best to turn them into Christians. I asked what sort of reception they got; the lady in charge said that most people were pleased to talk to them. and many had a deep desire to know more about what they taught. "The Catholics and Orthodox are much more active and seem to be able to reunite more people with Christianity than we do," she told me. She thought it was largely because of the cultural tradition the others had in the country from before the communist time.

That night over a long dinner we again met with Alex, the banker we had met on our first day in Tirana, who was anxious to know where we had been and what we had seen. He agreed that we had seen a surprising number of the best places in the country in our short visit—he was familiar with most of them, and as we talked about what we had seen and learned, confirmed that we had acquired largely correct perceptions about Albania.

I mentioned that we had noticed German and Greek banks in every town; Alex responded that these foreign banks had made major investments in Albania which had been a stabilizing force for the economy, a force that was badly needed. He reminded us about the nationwide chain-letter Ponzi scheme that nearly wiped out every dollar of savings in the country, that the banking and legal systems were slowly being rebuilt, but that there was still much to be done. He just smiled when I suggested that this was further evidence of what I had been told was the historical lawless so prevalent here. Annual per capita income, he told us, was about $3000, but some 80 percent of the economy remained underground and unreported, and foreign investment, other than the banks, was mostly limited to beachside hotels and condos, like those we had seen in Saranda. "How about foreign trade?" I asked. Most, he responded, was made up of the 15 percent of GDP remitted to relatives from citizens working abroad.

This had been a different sort of trip than the others, but it was nevertheless a fascinating week, and touched on many of the historical, religious, cultural, and geopolitical themes that we had experienced on our other journeys. The Albanians we encountered were a friendly lot—helpful, well-mannered, hospitable, and even pro-American. The American they love the most is George W. Bush, the only U.S. president who ever visited, whose name is found on bars and streets, and for whom a statue will soon be erected just outside of Tirana. Albanian leaders seem to have a centuries-old addiction to power struggles undertaken at the expense of the people, who would probably rather be left alone to raise their cows and their children. The people seem to accept, with good humor, the residue of their police state—an antiquated and almost feudal farming system, rusting factories and power plants, mostly built by the Chinese, and lots of those awful concrete block apartment buildings that communists were so fond of building across Eastern Europe. And they even accept, if begrudgingly, the fact that they were so abused by their dear communist leader for so many years. As one told me, when I asked him about it, "We were all spied on, but then we were all spies."

After forty-five years of brutal communist dictatorship and twenty years of struggling to undo it, Albania has finally begun to establish the outlines of a democratic government, the rule of law, and a free market. Although the country stands at a crossroads, even a short visit renewed our faith in the human spirit, and gave us hope that the culture will continue to reawaken and its people continue their return to faith as they rediscover what freedom means.

As our dinner came to an end I bid farewell to Nick and Alex and caught a cab to Mother Teresa Airport, where I spent the night in a very Albanian-modern hotel. The next morning I caught a 5 a.m. plane to Rome, and then back to Washington. Where, I wondered as I flew home, would we go next?

9

KRAKÓW TO ZAKOPANE TO KRAKÓW, POLAND

June 2014

POLAND IS THE MOST CHRISTIAN COUNTRY in Europe, boasting a long and proud alliance with the Roman Catholic Church that remains unrivaled anywhere in the world. It was the only Warsaw Pact country to maintain its deep faith from the end of World War II to the fall of communism in 1989; its culture survived through the faith of its people and largely, according to Polish Catholics, because of the Virgin Mary, who has played a unique role in Poland's history for 300 years. In 1717, Poland crowned the famous Black Madonna of Częstochowa as Queen of Poland. She has remained Queen ever since, and Poles claim she is responsible for the survival of the Polish culture through the nation's many trials—the great partition of Poland in 1795, the disappearance of Poland as a political entity from the Congress of Vienna in 1815 until after World War I, and the occupation and devastation of the country by both the Germans in World War II and the Soviet Communists after Roosevelt and Churchill handed it to Stalin in 1945. In 1955 the Poles were first to rebel against Soviet occupation, but the rebellion was brutally put down. To this day, Poland retains its anti-communism and hatred for the Russians, and its dedication to its Catholic faith.

I had last been in Poland in 1968, in the depths of the Cold War, while on a driving trip from Germany to Moscow, back through Ukraine, and ultimately to Budapest and Vienna. The trip took me across Poland, from west to east, with a couple of days in Warsaw. As was most of the Soviet Bloc in those days, it was grim, gray, and depressing. The people looked beleaguered and sad; the cities were largely composed of dilapidated old buildings and more dilapidated new ones—the ubiquitous concrete block apartment buildings. The countryside was made up of vast fields of not-very-good looking crops on the collectives, occasional peasants with ox-drawn wagons plodding along the road with a load of grain.

In 1968, I was recently out of college, and religion and faith were the furthest things from my mind. Although the Poles, dedicated Catholics that they were were battling the communists at every turn, I was oblivious to their fight. But by 2014, I was a fairly mature Catholic and a great admirer of Pope John Paul II. I had read and re-read *Witness to Hope*, George Weigel's wonderful biography of JPII. The Polish pope was a constant inspiration to all who served in the Reagan Administration— myself included—for his dedicated anti-communism. And, for me, as my life as a Christian matured, I found him to be an inspiration for my faith.

Statue of Pope John Paul II, Wadowice, Poland

In fact, it is probably safe to say that my decision to become a Catholic was influenced in no small part by John Paul II's consistent demonstration of unwavering faith in God and Jesus Christ. I recall being in an Episcopal Bible class of some sort in the mid-1980s, soon after I was baptized as an Episcopalian, and asking the priest, who was teaching the class—a rather renowned and popular fellow, considered a leader in the Episcopal community—what the Episcopal Church's position was on something, I do not remember what. "Oh," he said, "the Episcopal Church has no position on that. In fact, the Episcopal Church really has no position on anything." I was stunned and wondered how that could be. "That could not be true in the Catholic Church," I thought, at least as I observed what this courageous new Pope had to say about faith, about life, and about his Church.

So as Nick and I talked about taking a bike trip in Poland, the thought of going to Kraków where JPII had been the archbishop for many years, to Wadowice, his birthplace, and on to Zakopane, his favorite ski resort, seemed like such an obvious choice that I had to wonder why we had not done it earlier.

Since the disintegration of communism in 1989, Poland shined. The most prosperous of the old Warsaw Pact countries, it had joined the EU and NATO, had negotiated trade deals with many other countries, most notably its old archenemy Germany, which now manufactures auto parts, machinery, and many other products destined for export. The living standard is high, much of the country has been rebuilt and it is, all in all, almost a western European country. And Poland is almost unique in having maintained its staunch Christianity—Catholicism particularly—throughout World War II and the communist period. By 2014, when Nick and I began to consider it for our next pilgrimage location, Poland was considered the most Christian country in Europe.

Nick and I met in Kraków, the historical capital of Poland's culture and intellectual life, and where Karol Wojtyla had lived for forty years before being named Pope John Paul II in 1978 and had served as Archbishop since 1963. Over the next week or so we travelled on bicycles in a large circle south to Zakopane, Poland's most famous resort town near the Slovakian border, and back to Kraków, covering a swath of territory the Germans used to call Silesia. After a couple of squabbles with the bike shop, a couple of false starts, and after a day or two set aside for exploring Kraków, we planned to head off toward Wadowice, the little town where Pope John Paul II was born.

A friend in Washington, well-versed in Polish matters, had written to a friend of his, a graduate student named Marek at the Jagiellonian University in Kraków, who had agreed to show us around. We met him for a coffee on the Rynek Glowny, the main market square which, he told us, was the largest public square in Europe and just about the same size as the Piazza San Marco in Venice. Marek, a devout Catholic, was studying Polish history and was a font of information about the history and culture of Kraków.

"Kraków and Catholicism are inseparable," he told us. "You will see churches on every corner," he said, and indeed they were—full of flowers, often with music playing, crowds moving in and out and many people simply deep in quiet prayer, and Mass being said almost hourly. He took us into the Basilica of the Assumption of Our Lady, which dominated the square.

"At the end of the Communist period," he explained, "the church was almost black from pollution—you could hardly see the stained glass and the roof was covered with soot. But today, as you see, it is deep red, the stained glass shines, and the copper has been polished to a deep bronze." We entered to find a beautiful colored ceiling and an amazing wooden altar. "The Russians built a large steel plant just outside of town," Marek said, "which emitted so much pollution that the entire city was black with soot and the buildings deteriorating. It was closed soon after Poland was liberated, and Kraków has been almost completely cleaned up by now." With a broad smile, Marek told us that the steel plant was now a museum—"a museum to the failures of Communism."

This would be the first, and probably the most stunning, example I encountered on this trip, of the transformation from oppression to liberty, from suppression of the Church to religious freedom, and from the boorishness and vulgarity of Russian Communism to Polish culture. Polish artisans, Marek explained, had spent thousands of hours renovating this sacred place, which was now a symbol of faith, refinement, and the deep cultural traditions of Kraków. "It was in this church that Karol Wojtyla served as priest for nearly ten years in the 1950s. It was the worst decade of the Communist occupation, but Wojtyla never let them dominate him." He pointed out the confessional where Wojtyla sat every day, giving solace and advice to thousands of men and women and encouraging them to defy communist atheism and to pursue their life as devout Christians."

"What is it," Nick asked Marek, "that allowed Poland to survive communism as it did, as opposed to the other countries in the East Bloc?" Nick's question could not have been a better one for Marek. "It is our culture, which we never let the Communists change," he said. "The Church is the foundation of Polish culture. We never abandoned the Church, and the Church never abandoned us."

I asked him if the Church in Poland was having the same problems it was experiencing in Catholic countries of Western Europe, places like Spain and Italy. "It is beginning to suffer the pains of the twenty-first century and of modernity, but to a vastly lesser extent than in other Catholic countries of Europe," Marek responded. "Young families and single adults as well as the elderly still fill the pews, and Poland actually exports priests, particularly to Africa, Asia, and other former East Bloc countries," he said. He explained that each year, thousands of Poles make pilgrimages to Tyniec, often walking hundreds of miles over a span of a couple of weeks. "You should definitely stop there on your way to Wadowice," he advised.

Marek told us that during Lent, the Stations of the Cross take place publicly in virtually every city and town. Even in public policy, the Church's influence is profound: abortion, which was legal during the communist era, was banned in 1993, and the Polish constitution protects traditional marriage, while same-sex marriage and related matters simply do not exist on the Polish political map.

We spent several more hours with Marek. To me he was an inspiration, a lesson in what people can accomplish if they maintain their faith in God.

Kraków was teeming with nuns and monks, shops selling Christian items, and bookstores full of religious books. It is reported that 90 percent of all babies born in Poland are baptized and 90 percent of weddings are in the Church. And of course it is no secret that the Catholic Church played a major role in the overthrow of communism in Poland, and that during the communist period the Church was a huge thorn in the side of the regime. No small part of that thorn was the Catholic bishop of Kraków, Karol Wojtyla, later the Cardinal who was named Pope John Paul II in 1978 and ultimately sainted in 2014. John Paul II is now Kraków's most famous and beloved citizen, and his image appears everywhere in store windows and gift shops.

Marek was proud of his hometown, what it had accomplished since the demise of communism, and about its history as well. "Kraków was Poland's capital city until the end of the sixteenth century, when the capital was moved to Warsaw," he told us. "But it remained the cultural and spiritual center of Poland."

From the main square we walked up Wawel Hill, home to a medieval royal palace, the thirteenth-century Cathedral of St. Stanislaus and St. Wenceslaus, and many other beautiful old buildings which were part of the royal complex. This was the cathedral where John Paul had been Archbishop before he went to Rome. "A Mass will begin in a few minutes," Marek said. "Shall we stay?" It mattered little that it was all in Polish, as I knew exactly what was going on. The Anglican Nick seemed a bit uncomfortable, but took it all in stride. But to me, a Mass in John Paul II's church was enormously worthwhile. I was glad I was a Catholic, and proud to be one as well.

I made a subsequent trip to Kraków in January 2017 for a sort of master class with the Manhattan String Quartet, to play Beethoven's great quartet in E flat major known as "The Harp." During my visit, along with many quartet rehearsals, we had a certain amount of discussion of the history of Kraków, including an interesting account concerning the Poles and the Germans during the Second World War. The Germans seized Kraków in 1939 and made it their headquarters while they occupied Poland until the end of World War II. On the drive into the city from the airport, I could see an impressive and massive hotel sitting high on a cliff above the Vistula River. My cab driver explained it was built by the Germans in 1940 to house their officers. There isn't much other obvious evidence of the German occupation—the Poles disliked the Germans about as much as they later disliked the Russians, and whatever both occupiers left behind has been removed. But there is some other evidence of the German occupation in Kraków, and it is why I was invited to go there. And it is evidence that the Germans want to have it back.

As the Allies started bombing Berlin in 1940, German scholars determined that it would be wise to move valuable treasures—paintings, sculptures, manuscripts, old books and so on—out of Berlin to a place where they would be far from the fires that ultimately consumed most of the city. So they crated up tons of these treasures and hid them in churches in small towns in German-occupied Poland. At the end of the war, as Poland sunk into the communist East Bloc and the Poles realized that the communist leaders would likely pilfer the manuscripts if they were found, they moved over 500 wooden crates to the Jagiellonian University library in Kraków, where they remained hidden for nearly fifty years. When they were finally made public, after Poland was freed from the Communist government, the Germans demanded that they be returned. The Poles refused. Eventually, in these stashed archives, musicologists were astounded to find the original manuscripts of Beethoven's Seventh, Eighth, and Ninth Symphonies, and several of his quartets, Mozart's *Magic Flute*, *The Marriage of Figaro*, and *Cosi fan tutti*, several symphonies and works by Bach, Mendelssohn, Schumann, Brahms, Schubert and others, including Beethoven's "Harp" quartet.

I had yet to learn any of this during my 2014 visit to Poland—but I had plenty else to see and discover. We said goodbye to Marek, who had been a terrific guide and a fount of information, and rode along the Vistula, the river that flows through Kraków, on the top of a dam parallel to the river. The dam looked like something the communists would build, probably mostly by manual labor. Our destination was the Benedictine Abbey at Tyniec, about 20 kilometers from Kraków, which Marek had strongly recommended we visit. "The monks there have the reputation of being the friendliest monks in Poland," he told us. "They will greet you when you come in, and love talking to people like you—an American and an Englishman together will make their day. They would probably even enjoy having a glass of beer with you in the abbey restaurant."

Marek was right on the mark. A fairly young monk, probably in his thirties, whose English was excellent, took us in tow and showed us around. "Tyniec is still an active and thriving monastery," he explained, "and is famous across this part of Poland because of massive pilgrimages, particularly at Easter, when tens of thousands of people come for several days to celebrate the resurrection of Jesus Christ." He showed us pictures of a huge temporary campground, people eating at long tables, and most important, an outdoor Mass for several thousand people. I asked where they all came from. "From as far away as 100 kilometers. Most walk, often with their families, stay for two or three days, and camp out in the fields nearby. It is a sacred event for them and for us," he told us, "all done to honor Jesus Christ at the most holy time of the year." I asked why people came to this monastery as opposed to one of the others nearby, and he said it had been going on for hundreds of years, partly because of the abbey's reputation for joy and openness—but, he added, the joy and openness may also be results of the pilgrimage.

"How did the monastery manage during the Communist time?" I asked him. He explained that the monastery had barely managed sometimes, but was able to stay open continually.

"The Communists hated the monastery, hated the Catholic Church, and hated what we stood for," he said. "They saw all religion, and the Catholic Church in particular, as a threat to their totalitarian rule," he explained. "But if there was one person who was an inspiration to this place during those years, it was Karol Wojtyla. He always stood firmly against those atheists, and never let the Communists wear him down no matter how hard they tried—which was continuously. We are halfway between Kraków, where he was Archbishop, and his birthplace of Wadowice. He often visited here on his way back and forth—long before my time," he said, "but his presence lives on, almost as if he is still here."

Situated on a hilltop above the river, the abbey was founded in the eleventh century, was sacked by the Mongols in the thirteenth century and again by the Swedes in the eighteenth, but was rebuilt each time.

From there, we rode a few kilometers to Kalwaria Zebrzydowska (these names made me think I was back on the west side of Chicago), the location of the Calvary Monastery, another pilgrimage site famous for an image of the Virgin Mary which has been shedding tears since the seventeenth century and is supposed to perform miracles. The monastery is part of a larger park, dating from the early seventeenth century, which includes some forty-two chapels built to resemble the pattern of Calvary in Jerusalem, all connected by paths over a distance of about five kilometers. It is also a massive pilgrimage site, and the literature we were given boasts that over one million pilgrims come there a year—the second most visited pilgrimage site in Poland, after Jasna Góra (which we would visit a few days later). This place, only about fifteen kilometers from Wadowice, was another one of John Paul II's favorite stopping points on the way to and from Kraków, and his picture is prominently displayed there—as it is about everywhere in this part of Poland.

The park is also the site of a nationally known Good Friday passion play—a reenactment of the final hours of Jesus's life, complete with the procession up Calvary Hill, three men tied to crucifixes, Roman soldiers in full uniform, Mary at the foot of the Cross, all of which attracts thousands of people from across Poland.

The abbey at Tyniec and the Calvary Monastery spoke volumes about the Christian faith in Poland, and about the power of the Polish Catholic Church. I mentioned to Nick that no other place in the world could equal this—where millions of people put their everyday lives aside, travel dozens or even hundreds of miles over several days to honor Jesus Christ. With a smile, he commented that it was difficult to get British Anglicans to walk a block or two to church once a week.

The millions of pilgrims coming to this place reminded me of John Paul II's 1979 return to Poland, soon after he became Pope, where millions turned out to attend the Masses that he celebrated, and the absolute horror of the Communist elite as they watched the spectacle from booths with two-way mirrors. I asked one of the guides whether these pilgrimages went on during the Cold War and what the Communist reaction was. Indeed they did, he said—as intensely as ever.

We bicycled on about twenty five kilometers, through a deep pine forest to Wadowice, an obscure little place which suddenly became famous with the election of its hometown boy Karol Wojtyla to the papacy in 1978. A town of some 10,000 people—nearly one-fifth Jewish before World War II—and which probably had nary a tourist before Wojtyla became John Paul II, it is now a world tourist attraction. The pope's boyhood apartment and church, situated on John Paul II Square, are now the centers of attention. We went into the church, an imposing Baroque structure built and added onto over 500 years that includes several chapels, where John Paul II was confirmed and celebrated his first Mass. But the Wojtyla boyhood home was, unfortunately, closed for the day for some sort of repairs, to the chagrin of a long line of tourists, some of whom had undoubtedly come halfway around the world to see it. Still, there was plenty of other evidence of that most famous Pole's time in Wadowice. Including a statue of him just outside the church.

Without reservations, we had trouble finding a place to stay, but wound up in a charming little bed and breakfast managed by a lady of fifty or so, a native of Wadowice, who by the end of the evening was our great friend and a source of inside information about the Wojtyla family. She spoke no English, but her German was passable—although she was only willing to speak it when I assured her I was not a German. But an American? What could be better—she had relatives in Milwaukee, and maintained an active correspondence with them. Concerning the Wojtyla family, she told us that "in a town this size, everybody knows everybody." She said her mother grew up with Karol, who was the most popular kid in town. "He was an athlete, an actor, had a charming smile and every mother in town hoped that her daughter might be able to marry him, including my grandmother!" I asked if she knew him at all. "He was much older, but I did meet him a few times when he came back to Wadowice, which he did often, when he was the Archbishop. A wonderful, wonderful man."

Nick asked her about the reaction in Wadowice when they learned that he would be Pope. "Of course, it was the most incredible thing that happened here in a hundred years," she said. "In 1978 things were not good here. The Communists were cruel, there was little freedom. The Church was the only hope we had. But we knew Karol Wojtyla would not let the Communists push him around. We knew of his bravery, of his standing in the Church, so we were really not surprised. But of course we were! It was the happiest day of my life."

The next morning we rode south toward the Slovakian border. The terrain was becoming increasingly mountainous; the road went gently uphill along a river, but then turned toward the west and went up and down, up and down. After a long day of about 100 kilometers—which would not be bad if it had been level—we came to Zakopane, known as Poland's winter sports capital, on the edge of the Tatra Mountains and a few miles from the Slovakian border, a sort of Polish Aspen or Sun Valley. John Paul II, an avid skier, loved the place and, like every other town in that part of Poland, they loved him; his picture was everywhere, every gift shop had little statues, busts, post cards, hand-carved likenesses of every sort, and every other sort of trinket.

Nick mentioned as we rode along that the Zakopane area was known for its wooden churches. And sure enough, almost in the center of town we found a small church, the Church of Our Lady of Częstochowa, built entirely out of unpainted wood. Inside, the walls, floor, pews, and altar were a rich light brown natural wood. The sun was just going down over the mountains to the west and in the dusk and after 100 kilometers through hilly country on a bicycle, it seemed like the most peaceful place I had ever been. We said a quick prayer, and then got back on the bikes for a few miles outside of town, where we found several other similarly charming wooden churches.

We left Zakopane the next morning, not realizing that it was Corpus Christi, one of the great feast days in the Catholic Church and, naturally, a national holiday in Poland. I had gone out for an early morning walk, and as I passed a huge church, a Mass was about to start, and streams of people were going in. So I went in as well—it was a Monday—and was surprised to find the place packed, standing room only. I only learned that it was Corpus Christi when I asked the clerk in the hotel why so many people were in church on a Monday morning.

For one who has ridden thousands of miles on bicycles, that day stands out in my mind as the most exquisite and satisfying bicycle day of my life. It was a perfectly clear and warm June day; the scenery was picture-book perfect with most of the people dressed in fantastic peasant clothes— the women in striking colorful pleated dresses with white aprons and colorful headscarves, the men in tight fitting woolen pants, highly decorated with embroidered strips of colored cloth, decorative vests over white shirts with ruffled collars, handsome hats with great feathers, and knee-high leather boots.

Girl dressed in Polish Peasant's dress.

Nick and I took the ski lift to the top of the mountain adjoining the town, and then bicycled downhill for twenty five kilometers through beautiful, unspoiled valleys, past wooden churches and ski houses. Corpus Christi parades dominated the villages; it appeared that everybody in town was in the parade, all dressed to the hilt in full regalia—babies, children, and dogs in tow— tossing flower petals as they walked along. The churches and many houses were all built of logs adorned with carvings, designs, and decorations.

Corpus Christi Day Parade, near Zakopane, Poland

These were the Górale, a very independent group of moun-tain people, mostly farmers and, of course, devout Catholics who guard with their lives the century-old Polish traditions and culture that has died out across much of Poland (and who were a nightmare to the communists). They made up a considerable part of the Polish people who immigrated to the United States in the early part of the twentieth century. Although the area is a significant tourist attraction, the Górale seem oblivious to them and go about their lives in way that has not changed much, it appears, from the way it was lived for hundreds of years. As we bicycled down the mountain, we stopped at a small log church on the side of the road where several elderly peasants, in their full peasant costumes, waited for the Corpus Christi festival to begin. We fell into a sort of conversation with two women, dressed to the hilt in flowing flowered dresses, white aprons and the rest. Not a word of common language seemed to exist between us, but they were the sort of pilgrimage friends that we were becoming quite accustomed to making in our travels; about all that survived of the conversation, after explaining that I was an American, was the fact that one of the women had a son who lived in Chicago and that I was originally from Chicago. Ergo, we were instant soulmates.

We rode back toward Kraków for much of that beautiful Corpus Christi, through many more small towns, up and down hills, mostly on roads with no traffic. Every store, restaurant, and business was tightly closed, as everybody was celebrating that holy day. As we approached the little town of Czarny Dunajec, some 30 or 35 kilometers from Zakopane, we were suddenly in the midst of a parade through the center of town, ending at the local church. The parade seemed to include every man, woman and child, either in the parade itself or observing from the sidewalk, and every vehicle, horse, dog, coaster wagon, baby buggy, and the rest. All were dressed in those magnificent peasant costumes and most were carrying flowers and greenery. The local priest, carrying a large cross with a wooden carving of Jesus Christ, led the parade, followed by the altar boys, deacons, and an assortment of nuns and monks.

We biked on for another 20 or so kilometers, and eventually loaded our bikes onto a train back to Kraków.

The next morning we hired a car to take us to the monastery of Jasna Góra, home of the Shrine of Our Lady of Częstochowa— the "Black Madonna" and the "Queen of Poland"—eighty kilometers or so north of Kraków. The monastery is one of the great pilgrim destinations in Central Europe, and well over a million pilgrims walk each year from all over Poland to see the famous icon. Tens of thousands reportedly make the nine-day trek from Warsaw on Assumption Day in August. The day we arrived, we were just two of thousands of pilgrims, mostly Poles, straining to get a glimpse of the image of the Virgin Mary. The icon, according to Polish legend, was painted by St. Luke on a beam from the house of the Holy Family in Nazareth. Our driver, however, had a different account, telling us that it was more likely to have been painted in Italy in the fourteenth century. The icon is in fact very dark, which is probably from the black shading used by whoever painted it, and it continues to darken with age. Legend has it that thieves tried to steal the painting in about 1430, but as they started carrying it, it became heavier and heavier until they could carry it no further. Frustrated, they slashed the Virgin Mary's face with a knife; it started to bleed immediately, and the thieves fled in terror.

Jasna Góra has always been at the center of Polish resistance against occupiers, strengthened by the presence of the Black Madonna. This was particularly true during the Soviet occupation of Poland after World War II, and the size of pilgrimages there grew substantially—promoted by the Catholic hierarchy to demonstrate Polish patriotism and passive resistance to atheistic communism. Kraków bishop Karol Wojtyla was particularly devoted to the Black Madonna; when he was elected Pope in 1978, Jasna Góra received worldwide attention and remains one of the most-visited sites in Poland. A couple of years after my visit to Jasna Góra, I was chatting with my friend George Weigel, author of *Witness to Hope: The Biography of Pope John Paul II*, who told me when he visited Jasna Góra he was taken through parts not open to tourists and shown a guest book kept during the early part of the twentieth century. Among those who had signed the book in the early 1930s were A. Hitler and H. Himmler. After the German occupation of Poland in 1939, Hitler ordered all pilgrimages to Jasna Góra stopped, apparently recognizing the power that the Black Madonna had over the Polish people.

The Polish trip was a true pilgrimage—perhaps one of the best, real pilgrimages we had taken since Mt. Athos and the Camino. For me it was a wonderful combination of sensations. I had been to Poland during the depths of the Cold War, when it was grim, gray, and desolate; now, it was bright, happy, and thriving in so many ways. As a strong anti-communist myself, its survival of the forty-year blight was miraculous, particularly as compared to the other East Bloc countries I had visited, both before and after the 1989 Communist collapse. And as the home of John Paul II, that most admired Pope of my lifetime, it was an inspiration. But perhaps most of all, seeing these faithful people, living their lives to the fullest while maintaining their devotion to the Church, was a powerful reminder of the strength and depth of Christianity and of the Catholic Church—perhaps the most powerful reminder that I had experienced since my conversion ten years earlier.

10

BULGARIA

June 2015

THE TRIP TO POLAND had been a great success, both in terms of the physical challenge—bicycling through the countryside was exhilarating—but also in seeing how this very Catholic country had emerged from the devastation of World War II and nearly fifty years of repressive atheistic communist dictatorship into a free and prosperous country. So when Nick and I first started talking about another trip during the winter of 2015, I suggested another of the former East Bloc places, but one where we could experience the difference of how a country with a different religious tradition would compare with Catholic Poland. I suggested we go to Bulgaria—one of the more rarely visited Balkan countries, and a place certainly not on the average American's European circuit.

By 2014, I had travelled to each of the countries in the former East Bloc—other than those in the old Yugoslavia—except

Bulgaria. Several of those trips Nick and I had taken together, others I had done separately. Certainly off the beaten path, now the poorest country in the EU (and only a step or two ahead of Albania, which is not yet in the EU), and one of the forgotten Stalinist sisters, we agreed that Bulgaria was a logical destination. So Nick and I met at the airport in Sofia on a Saturday afternoon in mid-June 2015. We had no plan, no itinerary, only a couple of guidebooks and maps, a reserved hotel room in Sofia, and two bicycles we had arranged over the internet to rent.

East of Serbia and south of Romania, bordered on the north by the Danube, on the east by the Black Sea, and on the south by Turkey, Bulgaria has about seven million people in an area the size of Tennessee. Much of it is mountainous, although there are vast forests and plains in the center. It is a largely unspoiled place dotted by little villages and connected by windy roads. The language is totally unintelligible to an English-speaker, made worse by the fact that it uses the Cyrillic alphabet. Older people often speak Russian, not because of any linguistic similarity but because they had to learn it during the Cold War, and a few younger people speak some English.

Of particular interest to me was that Bulgaria was traditionally a Christian Orthodox country, which I thought would present an interesting contrast to the other former communist lands I had visited. It had also been high on the list of repressive regimes—not as bad as Albania, but much more so than Poland, Hungary, and Czechoslovakia. I had also read that the communist regime had virtually banned any religious activity shortly after taking power in the 1940s; although they loosened the ban somewhat in the successive years, they had also infiltrated the Orthodox Church, not unlike Stalin and his successors in the

Soviet Union had done. But apparently some of the Orthodox monasteries had survived, and Nick and I thought we would like to compare them to those we had seen in Romania and, of course, the monasteries on Mt. Athos—a couple of which, we recalled, were Bulgarian.

On our arrival, Sofia looked to us the way a typical former communist Eastern European capital looked in the nineties: shabby houses, broken sidewalks and curbs, abandoned buildings, holes in the streets, and dilapidated streetcars careening around corners, their bells warning bicyclists and pedestrians to get out of the way. And then there were the omnipresent massive Stalinist government buildings reaching to the sky, thoughtfully placed between hundred-foot-wide boulevards. There were several large Orthodox churches as well, but they looked about as shabby as the rest of Sofia.

Nick and I spent much of that first afternoon walking through the city, stopping at squares, churches, a café or two, and getting the feel of this very Balkan city. Eventually, we came to the Aleksander Nevski Cathedral, the home of the Bulgarian Orthodox Patriarch and one of the most noteworthy buildings in all of Bulgaria, thought of by the citizens of Sofia as its crowning glory. The church was built at the turn of the twentieth century in honor of 200,000 Russian soldiers killed in Bulgaria's 1877 War of Liberation. Dozens of domes and half domes are supported by hundreds of arched windows. The colossal interior, which can accommodate 5,000 worshippers (although it is hard to believe, given what we would later learn about Bulgaria's lackluster attitude toward Christianity, that more than a few hundred would ever show up) is covered with gold leaf, donated by the Soviet Union in the 1960s.

Nevertheless, the church is probably the most notable building in all of Bulgaria.

But there were some well-kept sections of the city, some large and fancy hotels, and a few expensive London and Paris shops. And, of course, the ubiquitous Mercedes and BMWs.

We reviewed the maps and guidebooks and a few websites over dinner. One site, in particular, described an eight-day organized bicycle tour of monasteries in the central part of the country, which we decided to try to follow on our own. The bikes arrived, as promised, at our hotel on Sunday morning— they were sturdy road bikes, well equipped and in good shape. We repacked our things into panniers, left the bags with the hotel concierge while promising we'd be back in a week, and set off to see Bulgaria.

St. Aleksander Nevsky Cathedral, Sopia, Bulgaria

I had read that train travel wasn't bad and that bicycles could always be taken aboard. But at the train station, we were still uncertain where we would go, and it was difficult to figure out which train went where. However, we discovered a large bus station next door to the train station, with buses seemingly travelling all through the country. After another review of the maps, we decided the bus was a better option and bought tickets to Ruse, one of the larger secondary cities, situated on the Romanian border and on the Danube about 100 miles or so from where it flows into the Black Sea. Ruse was in striking distance of the monastery route, and we thought there might be a decent bike path along the Danube—another alternative—as there was in Hungary, Austria, and Germany. Alas, no such thing existed.

The next morning we made our way out of Ruse to a "rock church"—a monastery and church literally built into a mountainside a hundred or so feet above the valley floor, accessible by a steep staircase carved into the cliff. This was one of five such churches, all designated as UNESCO Heritage Sites, in the vicinity of Ivanovo, built originally by hermits in the twelfth century and transformed into their present state in the fourteenth. The church consisted of several different rooms, all carved into the rock, the walls covered with paintings in an amazingly good state of repair It was still an active monastery, well preserved and cared for, although we personally encountered no monks. It appeared to be more of a museum than a church.

We proceeded along a small asphalt road, between a river and a cliff rising straight up for several hundred feet. Soon the road turned to gravel, later to dirt and eventually to grass; I was convinced that it was going nowhere, although Nick, with much laughter, urged that we continue onward. Sure enough, after much bumpy riding, mud, and long grass in the chains, we came out in a little village and back onto the main road. After about 30 or 40 kilometers and several long hills up and down, we came to Ivanovo, a very rural little place that could have been in Russia or about anywhere else in the old East Bloc.

The countryside was stunning—rolling wheat and grain fields as far as the horizon, a beautiful clear sky with larger mountains in the background, all giving the impression of an unspoiled and agriculturally productive country. But there were no villages for miles, just what might have been huge corporate farms. As we came into Ivanovo—a town of a few thousand people, at most—there were a couple of farm implement dealers selling massive John Deere and other combines, tractors, and other machinery, the sort you'd see in South Dakota.

Until World War II Bulgaria was a rich agricultural country, and more than half the GNP came from the land. When they came to power, the communists immediately seized the land and put it into massive collective farms, each with tens of thousands of hectares. Productivity immediately started to shrink, and by the 1960s productivity was about half of what it had been before collectivization, at which point the government allowed people to have small plots. The result, as elsewhere, saved the communists from earlier demise with a significant percentage of farm production coming from those small plots. After the fall of communism in 1991, the government attempted to de-collectivize the land, but met with great opposition from the local, still-communist officials, who destroyed records of earlier ownership and bribed farmers to not participate in the government plan. Eventually, these problems were overcome, and all the land we biked through in Bulgaria had been privatized.

To our surprise, the railroad ran through the middle of Ivanov, and as we rode next to the tracks, along came a train that looked like it had been built before the war and only painted with graffiti since. But it rumbled along, so we followed it to the station—a decrepit, old two-story building, but with an attractive enough outdoor café on the platform. Nick, ever the conversationalist, was able to strike up a relationship with the stationmaster and determined that the next train to Veliko Tarnovo, the city that appeared to be both an interesting historical place and the launch point for organized monastery bicycle tours, would leave in three hours or so.

With some time to kill before the train left for Veliko Tarnovo, we hopped back on the bikes to search for another rock church, which was supposed to be about ten kilometers away. The trouble was, it was at the bottom of a valley, which meant the ride down was exhilarating and restful, a fast trip with good wind in our faces but with the realization that it was going to be a long slug back. And the bigger trouble was, finding the church turned out to be beyond our capability. So, after much searching, we turned back disappointed to the long uphill ride back to the station.

Back in the café, as we were drinking another cold beer, an elderly couple across the way asked Nick, in perfect British English, whether he was from Kent. Close, he replied, but not quite. They were retired Brits who told us that they had bought a little house and piece of property nearby for—if I remember rightly—about 7,000 pounds and spent three or four months a year there, living for a fraction of what it would cost at home. I asked them how life was in the little town in Eastern Europe, as opposed to their traditional English life. "We just love it here," the wife said. "We are part of a regular community of other English couples who live in this town or others nearby. We often get together for dinner or little side trips, and as compared to the UK, it is a wonderfully inexpensive but beautiful, unspoiled country." They told us that hundreds, if not thousands, of Brits had done the same thing.

Eventually, more or less on time, came the rickety train, so we hoisted the bikes aboard and settled into a reasonably comfortable two-hour ride to Veliko Tarnovo.

Veliko Tarnovo is built on a series of steep hillsides separated by deep gorges; houses stand perched on the hillsides, sometimes one side being on a street sixty feet or more below the other. As luck would have it, the train station was at the bottom and the center of town at the top. After a couple of miles we came to the main square to find a tourist office. But it was just after six and what was obviously a closed sign hung on the door. Still, there was somebody inside, so after a sharp knock on the window the door opened and a friendly and smiling fellow in his thirties asked us in—in decent English—and asked if he could help. Immediately, he arranged for a hotel, gave us walking maps and guide books, took us to the hotel, this time downhill again, and agreed to come by the next morning and show us the town.

Veliko Tarnovo—at least the historic old town—was actually very scenic and well-kept; we passed many fine little shops and restaurants and tourists, and the view was beautifully scenic in the distance. We had a glass of wine with our new friend, named Roman, and immediately fell into conversation with a British couple at the next table who had, as our friends earlier in the day, also bought a small house nearby where they spent some weeks each year.

Roman met us the next morning, and we spent four or so hours walking about the town, going across a bridge to a huge castle and winding through crooked streets. "Veliko Tarnovo," Roman explained, "has a rich and long history. It was the capital of the medieval Second Kingdom from 1185 to 1396, finally wiped out by the Turks, and the site of the drafting of Bulgaria's first constitution in 1879." We walked in and out of many old Orthodox churches, most of which were in good condition, but relatively empty of people, and the ubiquitous craft shops, where craftsmen were making every conceivable kind of handwork, from jewelry, painted pottery, carved figures and much more. Roman told us about the large university in town, which made it, he said, a lively place. Roman was well versed in the history and delighted in drawing Nick and me into his Bulgarian world. But it was not only a history lesson: he also told us much about the current state of affairs, about the communist period, the culture, economy, etc. "Bulgaria has suffered from the brain drain that started after freedom was restored in the early 1990s," he said, adding that nearly two million young people, professionals, recent university graduates, and others had left the country (out of an original population of only nine million) leaving a very definite hole in the elite, intelligent, and professional class.

Nick asked about the state of the Orthodox Church. It was not much of a factor among younger people, Roman replied. "Services are largely attended by older people, and the church itself does not do much to recruit younger people," he said. As for the faith of the people, Roman, who said he was not particularly interested in church life himself, said they were not anti-religious, just ambivalent. "Would you consider most to be agnostic, then?" I asked. Probably a good way to explain it, he agreed. "For most

Bulgarians it just isn't much of a part of their lives."

By early afternoon we were ready to ride on again. First we rode to Petropavlovski Abbey (The Abbey of Peter and Paul), a small monastery, about 15 kilometers outside of town, along a busy highway. The monastery was still active, but barely. We went into the church, said a prayer, read what the tourist books had to say, and then continued up along the mountain road.

Soon the road turned down again, and in about 20 kilometers came to the monastery at Kilifarevo, a beautiful place next to a rushing river, emanating the sort of peace that only comes at such places of spiritual significance. Established in the eleventh century, Kilifarevo was one of the great cultural centers of the Slavonic world. Until the fourteenth century, it housed as many as 800 monks at a time, mostly scholars, who wrote books and translated the Greek and Roman classics into the Slavonic languages. But it was destroyed by the Turks, and rebuilt in the nineteenth century around the remains of an old church.

From what we could tell, the monastery had no more than a handful of monks. One shy and awkward fellow seemed to be in charge, who agreed that we could stay overnight in one of the cells—although we were the only guests, he insisted that we stay in the same room. Sleep—yes, but no food. Otherwise, he seemed to have no interest in talking to us, and seemed to have exactly the attitude that Roman had described earlier that morning.

The next day we went into the monastery chapel for morning Mass. The service was tedious at best. Our little monk friend was the only person in the church besides Nick and me, and he carried on the service, such as it was. However, in the Orthodox tradition, there were hundreds of paintings and icons of saints tacked to the walls. Nick explained that in fact our solitary monk, who was also the priest, was surrounded by hundreds of friends, and each one was deserving of a prayer or at least recognition in the prayer cycle. Part way through his prayers, the little monk stopped, walked to the side of the church and pulled, from a cubby hole, an electric iron, plugged it in, pulled a crumpled paper from his pocket, ironed the paper to remove the wrinkles and to coat it with wax. He put the iron away and returned to his prayer. We smiled at each other, decided we had heard enough, and went on our way.

We biked along a lonely and winding road next to a rushing stream, a cliff behind that—exactly the kind of road we had imagined we would find. But soon we turned uphill, to cross the mountain pass. For too many kilometers we pressed ahead, through beautiful and unspoiled forest in part of what signs told us was a Bulgarian National Park. Of course, we were rewarded as we crossed the crest of the mountain with a 10 kilometer downhill ride, S curve after S curve, through several small villages, and to a larger town at the bottom. We stopped at a little outdoor café for a cold drink—Coca Cola was everywhere and usually an invigorating choice after a strenuous uphill trek.

"So," I asked Nick, "what did you think of our latest monastery stay?"

Just about what Roman told us earlier, he said. "Perhaps well demonstrated by the fact that there was nobody but the priest in the church. Think of how that differs from the thousands of people who visit the Polish monasteries, not to mention the construction of new ones in Romania. This place had just one monk. One monk!" To what extent, we wondered, was this a reflection of the restrictive attitude of the Orthodox Church as opposed to the open and inclusive nature of Catholicism? We

surmised that the fact that the Bulgarian Communists had infiltrated the church, to make the people doubt its integrity and the
truth of its doctrine, was probably why it had so few followers.

As we chatted on, Nick asked me what I thought about post-
Communist Bulgaria as opposed to other places. "Somewhat
better than Albania," I responded. It was certainly cleaner, more
productive and had not had the economic panics Albania had
since 1990. "But as with the Church, certainly a long way from
Poland." We would continue to discuss these ideas for the rest
of the trip.

We again climbed another 8-kilometer mountain—more
of the same, followed by another long blissful downhill ride.
Eventually, we came to Tryavna, a beautiful little town, streets
lined with old wooden houses and several churches, including
some from the time of the Ottoman Empire, and dozens and
dozens of craft shops. Tryavna was the center of the Official
Guild of Master Builders and Woodcarvers in the seventeenth
and eighteenth centuries and descendants of the guild have
stayed on. Each shop was open, and the work produced was
of incredibly high quality. Even the houses were often covered
with carved wooden flowers and birds. Interestingly, however, the carvings and other crafts rarely had a religious flavor.
"Remember all the stuff we saw for sale in Poland?" I mentioned.
"Carvings of JPII, of Joseph and Mary, Jesus Christ, crucifixes,
images of churches, rosaries. Most had a Christian theme. Here,
virtually none do."

After several hours there and a fine late lunch in an outdoor café, we caught a train to Plovdiv—a three or four-hour
ride—the second largest city in Bulgaria. We arrived at about
9, in light rain, and found our way to the city's old town and

an attractive and friendly guest house, where we found rooms for the equivalent of about $12 a night, breakfast included. For us Westerners, I commented, Bulgaria was certainly a bargain. We got settled and went around the corner for a wonderful and leisurely late dinner and discussion. These trips are perhaps most rewarding for the long conversations Nick and I had—conservations which would make an interesting article if we could ever remember what they were about, but which were usually stimulating and well worthwhile. We had started talking about "big ideas" which, when they catch on, change some aspect of life or the world. Such diverse things as iPads, the development of cotton, and communism. We talked about violins and cellos, Mozart and Beethoven quartets. T. S. Eliot, Roy Campbell and the Sitwells, and the Orthodox Church all came into the conversation. And what about Christianity, I asked Nick. A lengthy discussion followed on that one—a continual conversation that followed us through this and all of the pilgrimages.

We awoke to a steady, driving rain—not a good bicycle day. But there was too much to see here to sit inside, so we put on our rain gear and proceeded to walk through old town Plovdiv. This was, indeed, an interesting place. First stop was a large house, now a museum, that was furnished as it had been in about 1890.

We were the only ones in the place, and the guide was most accommodating and helpful. The house had belonged to a wealthy merchant, probably the wealthiest family in Plovdiv, he told us. When he learned that we were an American and a Brit, he took us into what had been the owner's office, shut the door and, with a little smile that seemed to say, Don't tell anybody, removed the protective ropes across the chairs and asked us to sit down and be comfortable. The room, paneled in dark oak and furnished with heavy wooden European furniture, fit the mold of what such a place should look like. In rather tortured English, he told us that before World War I, Plovdiv had been the richest town in Bulgaria, the wealth largely based on trade which had developed over several centuries. There are traces of a Neolithic settlement there, he told us, dating to 6000 BC, and the city itself was founded 4000 years ago by the Thracians—it claims to be the sixth oldest city in the world. This fellow was a native of Plovdiv, he told us, had always studied the region's history, and was immensely proud of it. He explained that the city was built on seven hills and at the junction of two major rivers, Plovdiv was controlled by the Macedonian Greeks in the fourth century BC and later was a major Roman trading and cultural center. He suggested that we go down the street where we could find evidence of the Roman period. (We did go there after leaving this interesting house; in the middle of the main town square we found a Roman amphitheater, well restored and still used for concerts and theatrical events.) Our new friend related how the town had been passed back and forth between the Byzantine and Bulgarian Empires, and seized by the Ottoman Empire in the fourteenth century. Later, as we walked through the main square, we passed a collection of old churches from varying periods, all open for visits, but sadly, as in the rest of Europe, they were more museums than houses of faith.

One of the largest monasteries in Bulgaria—Bachkovo—lies about 35 kilometers from Plovdiv, and is one of the must-see destinations on a trip such as ours. But the rain continued and the road there was narrow, busy, and dangerous, and the last 10 kilometers or so was up a mountain, through several tunnels, and not a good place for a couple of aging bicyclists. So, we decided to take the bus. After a rather protracted argument with the driver about whether he would allow us to put the bikes in the luggage bin under the bus, we prevailed and soon arrived near the monastery.

Bachkovo is one of the largest and oldest Eastern Orthodox monasteries in Europe. Known in Bulgarian as the Monastery of the Mother of God, it was founded in 1083 and became a cultural and religious center, with a school that taught mathematics, literature, history, music, and probably most of the other subjects that American university students now avoid. The monastery was sacked and destroyed by Turkish Muslim invaders in the fifteenth century but was largely rebuilt over a couple hundred years. One building, the ossuary, somehow escaped the Turks' attention and still stands today, several hundred yards away from the main complex.

The cathedral, rebuilt after the Turkish invasion in the early seventeenth century, is still intact. We were met at the door by an elderly man who offered to give us a tour, show us the icons, explain the architecture, etc. One icon of the Virgin Mary, he explained, has supernatural powers and attracts thousands of pilgrims each year. I quipped to Nick that they must come on a different day than this one, as we were the only pilgrims there.

The only other things missing were the monks. Bachkovo probably had as many as 1000 monks at one time, and if it were on par with the Bulgarian monasteries we had seen at Athos in Greece, probably had that many, perhaps more, until World War I. But now? There were a few, perhaps a dozen or so. Otherwise, this massive place was deserted.

How it differed from the monasteries we had visited in Bukovina in Romania, where the cloisters were so overflowing with monks and nuns that new facilities were being built from the ground up, and where churches had been restored and were full of worshippers. Even in Albania—a nation with a three-way mix of Orthodoxy, Catholicism, and a mild form of Islam— religion seemed to be much more vibrant than here in Bulgaria.

Albania, Romania, and Bulgaria had been the three most repressive communist countries during the post-World War II period until the blessed collapse of communism in 1989. Nicolae Ceauşescu, head of state in Romania, and Enver Hoxha, dictator in Albania, had done everything in their power to suppress any trace of religion, although Albania had been even more severe than Romania, passing a statute that mandated atheism. Both killed thousands of religious people, razed religious facilities and persecuted and imprisoned others short of killing them. But Bulgaria was different.

Bulgaria, historically, was one of the most Orthodox European Countries, the church encompassing virtually the entire population. In the first century, the Apostles Paul and Andrew brought the Christian faith to Bulgaria, and the Orthodox Church itself has dominated Bulgaria ever since, at least until the Communists took control. There were, at one time, a couple hundred monasteries (of which forty or so are still open, in one way or another); there were, and still are, churches in every village and neighborhood, and the Church had once wielded vast influence over everything that happened.

When communists seized power after World War II, Bulgaria initially had a couple of short-lived communist leaders, until 1949 when Todor Zhivkov, a confirmed Stalinist, was made head of state. Rather than try to obliterate the Church, he adopted the Soviet model and went about subverting and controlling it: some priests and other religious leaders were assassinated, probably largely to get the attention of the rest; the civic functions of sacraments such as birth and death certificates and marriages were transferred to the state, and all priests were forced to sign a declaration that they agreed with the dictates of the state. If they refused, they were either defrocked or killed. Bulgarian KGB agents then began infiltrating the Church; some were even ordained. Disinformation about the Church was disseminated and, in the best tradition of communist intelligence, the Church slowly became irrelevant and distrusted by the population. A majority of the members of the Orthodox Church's Holy Synod were actually members of the Bulgarian state security apparatus, meaning that the Church in Bulgaria was little more than a branch of the atheistic Communist Party.

That is no doubt why, even long after the communists had been removed from power, we found that Christianity was so moribund in Bulgaria. Where the Church had been forcibly shut down, priests, monks, nuns and other religious figures publicly executed, churches razed and outlawed, people were anxious to return once the horror ended. But in Bulgaria, the mistrust and the cynicism sewn by communist subversion lingered on, and will perhaps for generations.

After a time praying in the cathedral, we found the monk in charge of rooms and arranged to stay over. The dormitory was huge—the hallways perhaps a hundred or more feet long, with dozens of rooms on each side. The room itself was Spartan: a cot, a little table and chair, a 20-watt light bulb hanging from a wire. The bathroom, such as it was, was at the other end of the corridor. No hot water, no towels or toilet paper, and a couple of those Arabian-style, hole-in-the-floor toilets with the little places to put your feet. Luckily I didn't have to use it.

Several weeks after I returned home, I was suddenly attacked by a gastrointestinal bleed and rushed to the emergency room. I lost fifteen pints of blood, had as many transfusions, and ultimately had major abdominal surgery. As I recovered, I could only thank God that it had not hit me in that grim little room in Bachkovo Monastery, fifty kilometers from the nearest town. Who knows what sort of conveyance might have been available to get me to medical help, or even if there was a telephone that could summon an ambulance, and who knows what sort of medical facility I might have found. I shudder to think about it.

We started off at about six the next morning—as soon as the gates of the monastery opened, and proceeded back to Plovdiv. Traffic was relatively light, the weather was clear, hills were pointed down and we hurried along and spent the rest of the day riding back toward Sofia—on level backroads, with no traffic, mountains in the distance, skies blue. After about 80 kilometers, we caught a train for the rest of the way in Sofia.

Nick and I had a long dinner—at the same restaurant we had found on our first evening—reminiscing about the trip. As we ate a plate of mixed grilled meats (a Bulgarian specialty), we drew observations and conclusions about what we had seen. The bicycling, we agreed, was exhilarating. Mostly on back roads, beautiful scenery and lots of ups and downs, we had covered nearly 400 kilometers. As we always did, we complimented each other on the fact that we had found an interesting and fulfilling route across this far-away country, had always found places to stay and to eat, and had experienced no mishaps of any kind. I mentioned that we were getting pretty good at these pilgrimages and with enough years, could cover the rest of the globe.

Reliving the history on this pilgrimage, particularly the period between World War I and the collapse of communism, was always a thrill and confirmed much of what I knew from my extensive study of that period in Eastern Europe.

But most interesting was the difference that we found in Bulgaria from our most recent trip to Poland and our earlier trips to Albania and Romania. Clearly, Nick mentioned, Catholic Poland was so obviously different than Orthodox Bulgaria because of their respective church traditions. And Albania, a mix of Orthodoxy, Catholicism, and Islam, where all religion had been banned for nearly fifty years, was in a different category. But Romania? Also an Orthodox country, but at least in Bukovina, where we had visited the painted churches several years earlier, Orthodoxy was thriving. Nick explained that all Western Orthodox churches held the same beliefs, the same traditions, and the same culture. "One Lord, one faith, one baptism" is their tradition. In the end, we surmised, the difference was probably due largely to the culture and the way the Communists had subverted the Bulgarian Church to their ends—creating distrust and doubts among the population which still lingered on. "A tactic the Left still uses on many fronts," I remarked to Nick.

As a footnote to our pilgrimage, we congratulated each other that we had made it through another long trip without an argument or disagreement. Neither of us knew of anybody else with whom we could make such a trip.

Early the next morning, I started the long flight back to Washington.

11

FOLLOWING ST. PAUL ON THE VIA EGNATIA

Greece, June 2017

THE FIRST ROAD TO CONNECT ASIA AND EUROPE, the Via Egnatia, was built 200 years before the birth of Christ. Starting in Byzantium on the Bosporus, somewhere near what we now call Istanbul, it stretched for over 1000 kilometers across Macedonia (now Northern Greece) and eventually up the Albanian Adriatic coast to connect with other roads that went on to Rome. It was used by armies—the Romans transported lots of them—as well as merchants, bureaucrats, and travellers of every other sort. But it also moved ideas, philosophies, religions, and everything else the Romans carried with them from one place to another.

It is still there, after 2200 years. Of course, some of it has been paved over or torn up. Rocks have been used for foundations and walls, and stretches have been eroded away. But parts of it are more or less the way the Romans built it, and other parts still very passable in the forms of paths, gravel or asphalt roads. Even the main street running through Thessaloniki, the second largest city in Greece, is part of the Via Egnatia.

As we spoke in January about another trip, Nick suggested going to Greece to follow the Via Egnatia. We had seen a bit of it in Albania in 2012, and Nick had done a little research to discover that it was something of a trail that hikers, bikers and others were following, with the added attraction that several significant biblical sites were on it—including Philippi, Macedonia, and Thessaloniki—and that Paul had travelled along it several times.

The Paul connection was especially interesting. After Jesus himself, Paul is perhaps the most interesting and influential person in the Bible. We had encountered his tracks on previous trips, first in Ephesus and later in Assos (both in Turkey), and again in Damascus, and had probably crossed his paths another time or two. It therefore would be not only intriguing but also fitting for us to visit some of the places in Greece where he had been and to learn more about what he did while we explored the actual sites where he travelled, preached, and taught.

Nick had also come across what looked like the London or Washington subway map, but which was actually a map of Roman roads, the Via Egnatia prominently included. As I looked at it, I thought it would be interesting to travel for some distance on one of these roads to get a sense of the network that the Romans built and what travelling on them was like.

Our first trip, of course, had been to Mt. Athos in Greece—a trip which had been a sort of foundation for all the others—and although we did not know if 2017 would be our last, we agreed that a trip to another part of Greece might be a fitting bookend to the entire enterprise.

So we decided to follow as much of the Via Egnatia on bicycles as we could in a week. But as on our other trips, that is about all we planned, trusting that once again we would be able to come up with a plan once we arrived at the starting point.

On my trip in from the airport, I was lucky enough to get a cab driver who spoke virtually perfect English. He introduced himself as Dmitri and told me he had worked for several years in Chicago before returning to Athens. Dmitri was full of information. He asked what I would be doing in Greece, and when I told him that I would meet a friend and we would bicycle along the Via Egnatia, he immediately suggested places to go and to avoid. His family, he told me, raised fruit 100 or so kilometers west of Thessaloniki along the route, which was one of the most scenic and peaceful areas of Greece. "Better to take a train west and ride back than to the east," he said. "The scenery is better, the towns are better, and although hilly, the road back to Thessaloniki will go downhill along the coast." If we went to the east, he said, we would get to Philippi, one of the most interesting cities in Greece, but the landscape getting there was flat and boring. Good advice, I told him.

As we drove along, we passed a large Orthodox church—it was a Sunday—with hundreds of people just coming out of a service. I told him I was curious about the state of the Orthodox Church in Greece and whether Greece was experiencing the same sort of drain so prevalent in Western Europe. He explained the Church there was still in good shape—"Perhaps not as good as thirty years ago," he admitted, "but a far cry from the Catholic Church in Western Europe." He said Greece remained a strongly

Christian country, that many people were devout followers of Orthodoxy, and that it was virtually the state religion. I asked if younger people remained devout. Religion was part of the school curriculum, he told me, so that therefore nearly every Greek citizen was essentially raised in the Church. I later confirmed that literally 90% of Greeks consider themselves members of the Orthodox Church. "What about Muslims?" I asked. He smiled as he said that Muslims made up not more than 2 or 3% of the population, and even those had a tough time finding a mosque. Recalling our experience in Athos, where it was clear that Catholics were not welcomed, I decided not to jeopardize our rapport by asking about the state of Catholicism in Greece.

A gas station on the side of the road was teeming with Arab-looking young men, all poorly dressed and very sloppy looking. Dmitri pointed to them and told me they were immigrants from across the Mediterranean. "We read about them in the papers at home," I replied, and said I assumed there are plenty of them in Greece. Some in Athens, he answered, but most are on the islands off the coast. And on some of them, hundreds of thousands. He did not think we would run into many on our trip along the Via Egnatia.

Finally, as we were coming into central Athens, I asked him about the economy, whether it was as bad as we read in the news at home. "Probably worse," he said. "I am only driving this cab because I can get no other job, and am lucky to be able to do this." Unemployment, he said, was around 25%, higher among young people. He mentioned that just the day before, thousands of students had protested, some violently, because the government was planning to raise university tuition, which until then was free. "We all hope the Germans will bail us out," he said. "But I am not sure why they would."

Athens is a teeming and unattractive city of nearly six million people—half the population of Greece—built in no apparent pattern, with streets going every which direction, too many cars and bikes, and lots of pollution. Except for the occasional church or ancient monument, the houses and apartment buildings all look like they were built since World War II—and in fact many were, as the city was largely destroyed when the Germans occupied Greece and in fierce fighting during the war between the British and Germans.

I met Nick that hot and rainy Sunday afternoon at Theodotou Square in central Athens. We hadn't seen each other since a quick meeting in New York a couple of months earlier, and after greetings and catching up over a cold beer we stepped into the Church of the Pantanassa, a tenth-century former monastery. A service had just ended and the place was packed, even on this humid afternoon.

We walked up the Acropolis, the hill visible from almost any point in Athens and the site of the Parthenon. Everyone has seen pictures of this ancient Greek temple and read about its history and importance, but nothing compares to standing there and looking up at this incredible building. It was built in the fourth century BC and is considered the apex of what remains from Ancient Greece and the Doric order. As our trip progressed we would see many of the origins of Western Civilization, and I mentioned to Nick that I thought the Parthenon—aside from the Christian Church—is probably the single most important symbol of democracy and what the West would come to stand for.

An official-looking guide was walking around, so I approached her and asked if she spoke English or German.

English, she answered, so I inquired about the restoration which was so evidently going on. She told me that it was being paid for by the EU and had been underway for the past twenty years or so. "It is beginning again to look the way it must have before its incredible history of sacking and destruction" she responded. "The wars, invasions, and occupations by Italians, Venetians, Ottomans, Germans, and others, the sacking of stone, figures, tiles, et cetera, practically destroyed this historic place." She explained that over the years it had been a Greek temple, an Orthodox Church, a Catholic Church, a mosque, and a powder magazine (resulting in almost complete destruction in the late seventeenth century)." Nick added, looking at the mobs of tourists, that it was apparently the destination for millions of Western European and Japanese tourists. "Indeed it is," the guide responded. Greece, she explained, gets twice as many tourists every year as the entire population.

The engineering and architecture required to build this temple astounded me, as they would at many of the sites we would visit throughout the trip. Built 500 years before Christ, the building is over 200 feet long and 100 feet wide. The dimensions and the proportions look to be perfect, as if they were designed by the most sophisticated computers and instruments. The columns—forty-six around the outside and twenty-three inside—are nearly six feet in diameter and each weigh several tons. They were constructed with incredible precision: rather than having a perfect taper, as they appear, each column has an eighth of an inch bulge to offset the optical illusion that they are not straight. Neither do the columns stand straight up and down, but just an inch or two off, better to support the marble roof. Would that buildings were built with such precision and care today, rather than the monstrosities we erect and tear down a decade or two later.

We flew to Thessaloniki the next morning and picked up the rented bikes—high quality Italian road bicycles that would suit us well. Over dinner the night before, we had mapped out a potential journey along the Via Egnatia—the choice was either to go east from Thessaloniki toward Turkey and back, or west toward Albania and back. Taking the advice of Dmitri, the cab driver, we chose the latter; we decided we would take a train as far toward Macedonia as we could go and ride back to Thessaloniki. It was a good choice, as it turned out, as Thessaloniki is at sea level, and although there would be plenty of hills up and down, Thessaloniki was about 3,000 feet lower than the end of the line.

Negotiating Thessaloniki traffic while trying to read the street signs in Greek turned out to be a challenge, but we found the railroad tracks (Greek railroads hardly match the Bundesbahn) so we followed them to what looked like the station and rode right in on one of the platforms. It wasn't the station, however, but the repair shop, with railroad cars and engines in various state of disrepair. A group of Greek men, sitting around a disassembled car and drinking tea, found our entry on bikes terribly amusing, and with lots of laughter directed us to the next facility down the line which was, in fact, the station.

Nick went off to find the ticket counter while I watched the bikes. Two trains a day, he reported, went to Florina, our destination and the end of the line; one had already gone, the second was in an hour, but according to the ticket agent, only the first could accommodate bicycles, the second could not. Everything, I concluded, is negotiable, so I went back to the ticket agent (an attractive blond had just replaced the older fellow who Nick had spoken to) and sweet-talked her into letting us take the forbidden bikes on the next train. "OK with me," she let me know in broken English, "but you will have to check with the supervisor." Having heard that everything in Greece is for sale, I offered him twenty Euros. I was stunned when he laughed and wouldn't take it, but ultimately he agreed to let us bring the bikes.

From Florina, we proceeded down back roads and through spectacular fruit farms, through a border crossing, complete with armed guards and passport inspections left over from Cold War days (Macedonia is neither in the EU or NATO and maintains its proud independence) into Macedonia and to Bitola, our first stop on the Via Egnatia.

Northern Greece was known as Macedonia for centuries, and it is no small irritant to modern Greeks to have this tiny upstart of a country of some two million people call itself by what Greeks consider their name—especially since modern Macedonians are Slavic people who speak a Slavic language and were part of Yugoslavia until the fall of communism in 1991. (It is the only Yugoslav country to have departed without a war.)

Macedonia is a mishmash of Orthodox Christianity, a bit of Catholicism, and Islam—although not very serious Islam—left over from the Byzantine and Ottoman periods. Bitola is home to mosques and Christian churches, which stand peacefully next to each other, neither taking themselves or the others very seriously.

Although not actually in Greece, Bitola had acquired a good many Greek habits, not the least of which was that about every other storefront is a bar or restaurant, all with tables outside, usually under great umbrellas to protect from the rain, and set so that the customers are facing toward the street, as if they were posed to have their picture taken with the restaurant as backdrop. And virtually all of these customers were middle-aged men. Five or six would gather around a table, ogle the pretty girls going by, drink wine, play dominoes, discuss politics and international affairs, and enjoy life to its fullest.

We rode out of Bitola to the East, toward Thessaloniki and Istanbul. Just on the edge of town, we had our first encounter with the Egnatia: the old road ran through the center of Heraclea Lynchets, an ancient city founded in the fourth century BC by Philip II, Alexander the Great's father. The ruins had been well excavated and preserved, the work beginning in the 1930s, interrupted during the War, and continuing into the present. We were the only tourists; the guide showed us around and directed us to the best parts of the town, and after a few minutes told us to just wander around at will. "What you see here," he told us, "is about 10 percent of the ruins which can be found from one end of Bitola to the other...it was a dynamic and central part of the Empire in the early days." There is much more of Heraclea to be discovered, it is believed. Large mosaic floors had been preserved—all without the typical signs warning tourists not to walk on them—in addition to temples, shops, and a large amphitheater that easily could have seated 3,000 or more people. The theater, which was only discovered and unearthed after World War II, includes animal cages and tunnels under the spectator section opening onto the theater section; historians speculate that there were undoubtedly some fairly bloody exhibitions during Roman times. Unlike so many of these cities, the Heraclea ruins are virtually unrestricted, so we were free to climb around on the rocks, up the theater, and wherever else we decided to go.

We walked along the Via Egnatia in Heraclea for a few hundred meters; the road was visible and passable on foot but not on bicycles. The stones were uneven and rough, and the road appeared to disappear into a rough path before the stones appeared again after another hundred meters. So we rode along a paved country road that ran parallel, and headed on to Edessa through the fantastic mountainous countryside, fertile valleys, and farmland, and back through the same border crossing we had crossed earlier, this time entering Greece.

Edessa sits high on a hill looking across a great valley toward Thessaloniki. Known as the city of waterfalls, several rivers plunge over the cliff at the edge of town, cascading down into the valley and on to the Aegean a hundred or so miles away. The city, which has been around since well before the Romans arrived at about the time of Christ, is well preserved and as attractive as could be.

We stopped at an outdoor café overlooking a waterfall that fell several hundred feet into the valley below. Edessa, Nick explained, was the home of some of the earliest Christians— probably about 200 AD. It was captured by the Byzantines and the Ottomans and remained under Arab rule for several centuries, with the exception of a couple of hundred years in the twelfth century, when it was held by Crusaders. Significant Arab influence is still evident in the architecture, and several mosques remain, although the population is now largely Greek.

The Via Egnatia runs through the center of Edessa, very visible in certain places. Scholars think Paul probably came through Edessa in about 55 AD, on the third of his missionary journeys, after he left Ephesus and on his way to the Adriatic coast, where he took a boat to Italy. But if he did, we could find no evidence that he had. Just outside, we found another large Roman town where major excavations had been undertaken— the site must have been at least a square quarter mile or more, without another tourist in sight. After an hour or so, we biked on to Giannitsa, a rather large and well-kept town.

Over the course of the next several days, we visited several more of these ancient cities; some had been more excavated than others, some were still in a primitive state. The two which were the most spectacular and representative of all the others were Pella and Philippi. Both had major excavation projects, mostly starting sometime after World War II, and each must have involved hundreds of people working tens of thousands of hours. The result is truly amazing.

Pella was the capital of the Kingdom of Macedonia during the reign of Alexander the Great. It was then a port city, but the inlet leading to it has since been silted over. There is reference to the city as early as the fifth century BC; it was the birthplace of both Phillip II and his son, Alexander the Great, born in 356 BC. It was sacked by the Romans in the second century BC and ultimately destroyed by an earthquake in 90 BC. In the meantime, it was a place of incredible grandeur.

It was evident that the city was built on a grid of thirty-foot-wide streets, the blocks being some 150 by 300 feet and covering some 300 acres, or about a third the size of Central Park. Along this grid lay thousands of houses, some quite grand, together with shops, temples, athletic sites, theaters and amphitheaters, almost comparable to a modern city. Many of the houses had piped water and sewer, and many had frescoes and mosaic floors, several of which are preserved in the ruins and in the museum close by—which was, in its own right, one of the best museums I have ever seen. Built in 2009, it was modern, clean, light, and beautifully laid out. It housed positively the most astounding collection of antiquities and artifacts all found at Pella: room after room of statues, carvings, stone work, mosaics, and artwork of every variety. One of the most interesting exhibits was one showing day-to-day life in ancient Pella, including the inside of houses, shops, workshops, and offices. For a country as broke as Greece, it is astounding that money was scraped together in sufficient quantities to build such a spectacular edifice.

In the center of Pella stood the Agora which covered some ten city blocks, or nearly twenty acres. Here was the heart of the city—administrative offices, shops, some apartments for high ranking officials, markets, and temples. The foundation is preserved, and enough still exists that the grandeur of the building is reproduced in the museum.

Paul, according to a booklet I picked up at the museum, had come along the Via Egnatia on his second missionary journey, but had turned off before getting to Pella to go to Berea, a few miles away. From the accounts we found, there was virtually no Christian activity at Pella. Of course, it was a Greek city, founded well before the birth of Christ, and the religion there was dedicated to worship of the Greek gods.

Nick and I did walk on the remains of the Via Egnatia for as far out of Pella as we could find the actual Roman road. On a hot, Greek June day—probably close to 100 degrees Fahrenheit—the thought of walking for hundreds of miles, as Paul and thousands of others did, is exhausting to even think about. It is estimated that going from Byzantium to the Adriatic, in what is now Albania, would have taken about twelve weeks of walking six days a week and resting on the Sabbath. The alternative would have been to take a series of boats, which could have taken, depending on the weather, nearly twice as long. Paul would stop in every town to preach the Gospel, to encourage whatever believers he could find, and to try to form a church. Several days after our Pella visit, in Philippi, we would find more evidence of his efforts.

The Via Egnatia ran through the center of Pella, and was, in fact, the main avenue through the city. From there it went on through a great, wide valley filled with beautifully nurtured orchards and truck gardens, to Thessaloniki some 80 kilometers away. We decided to do it as quickly as we could, only stopping for a cold drink from time to time. As we got closer to Thessaloniki—a major metropolis, the second largest in Greece—the Egnatia became a busy four-lane highway without much of a shoulder. But we moved along as fast as we could, arriving in Thessaloniki in late afternoon.

The bike shop was situated on the grounds of the Makedonia Palace Hotel, a modern and well-appointed five-star hotel right on the large bay on which Thessaloniki is built. Our lodgings so far had been quite rudimentary, at best, so we thought we would splurge and stay in this modern, first-class place. I pulled up a hotel booking website, and sure enough, two rooms were available. After dropping off the bikes, therefore, and still dressed in our biking clothes (which meant shorts and a polo shirt—no spandex bike suits for us), we started into the hotel.

"Not so fast," a policeman at the gate said, and suddenly we were surrounded by Greek cops, security guards, what looked like a SWAT team, and about forty of the toughest-looking goons you can imagine. They were Israelis, as it turned out, there to protect the visiting "Bibi" Netanyahu, who was also staying at the Makedonia Palace Hotel. After a thorough search of everything we had, we were let past the security barriers and proceeded to the front desk. I could not resist pointing out to the clerk that we had just reserved rooms twenty minutes earlier, and yet they had put all this security together in so little time just for us?

The trip, so far, had been a delight, and everything worked out to a T, but it hardly resembled a pilgrimage. Aside from Thessaloniki, we had seen virtually nothing of St. Paul, who had played such a major part in this part of the world, and who had a good deal to do with the fact that we were here at all. So we rented a car and drove east, toward Istanbul, again along the Via Egnatia. But in this area, the ancient road had been transformed, obviously with vast amounts of EU money, into a super highway which rivaled anything in the US—though almost completely devoid of traffic. We followed this route to Philippi, which lay one hundred sixty or so kilometers east of Thessaloniki.

St. Paul travelled along many miles of the Via Egnatia with Timothy and St. Luke; he landed, on his second missionary journey, in about 49 AD in Neapoli, now known as Kavala, and travelled the short distance to Philippi. From there he walked on to Thessaloniki, probably travelling further west in the direction of Pella. It was indeed ironic that this peaceful man, whose life was devoted to spreading the story of Jesus Christ, whose letters make up a substantial portion of the Bible, and who is probably more responsible for spreading the Gospel of Christianity to the Western world than any other person short of Christ himself, travelled along this Roman military road—one of the most important thoroughfares of one of the most bellicose cultures in history. But without the ability to travel Paul would not have encountered the churches he wrote to, the churches which formed the foundation of his writings and his theology. Paul had to reach beyond his immediate horizons, both literally and figuratively. Without the Via Egnatia, travelling from Asia across what is now Greece and Macedonia would have been impossible for Paul.

In Philippi, we could follow in Paul's footsteps. The ancient city is thirty or so kilometers inland, lying on a vast plain and against a steep and rocky mountain—the sort of place Greeks often chose for their cities for obvious reasons. As we drove across the plain, as flat as it could be, we realized that it was here that the Roman Republic, in 41 BC, met its demise in the great battle between the forces of Brutus and Cassius versus Antony and Octavius. After a few false turns and roundabouts, we were suddenly in the parking lot of the ancient city, complete with an attractive restaurant and park.

The Via Egnatia runs through the center of Philippi, as it did in Pella; here it was made of huge flat stones laid some 2300 years ago and still in better shape than many western roads despite ruts from thousands of chariot and wagon wheels. The old city is four meters or so below the level of the earth. The French, after World War II, took it upon themselves to excavate this place, so that what Nick and I were in the midst of was the skeleton of the ancient city—foundations, rain gutters, the bases of columns, with paving stones running between the excavations. We walked along Roman baths, basilicas on both sides of the street, temples, a Roman forum, a fourth-century theater which the Romans renovated for gladiatorial contests, remnants of several Christian churches, and an acropolis.

As we walked toward the center of the old city, we suddenly came upon an incredible sight: the remains of a Byzantine basilica. On the drive from Thessaloniki, I had read that before the French archaeologists arrived, it was the only thing sticking out of the earth and was believed by the locals to be some sort of triumphal archway. In fact, it was a Greek cathedral which is believed to have been dedicated to St. Paul.

Before the trip I had decided to read *In the Steps of St. Paul*, by the great twentieth-century Anglican writer H. V. Morton, who had visited Philippi in his studies of St. Paul's travels. He wrote about the visit in descriptive terms:

> As I sat in these lonely ruins, I was able to build a picture of the Philippi that St. Paul, St. Luke, Silas and Timothy saw when they came along the Via Egnatia from Neapolis. The old town which Philip of Macedon, Alexander [the Great]'s father had founded, climbed the acropolis hill; its streets were steep, its houses were old and Greek-looking, its temples, flashing in the sun, were a shining landmark for miles. On the flat land at the foot of the hill was the new Roman colony which Augustus had founded, very Roman, very official, very proud, full of old soldiers…

There was no synagogue in Philippi, as apparently there was a dearth of Jews. Paul and his apostles needed a place to pray so, according to the account in Acts, they "went forth on the Sabbath by a river side where we supposed there was a place to pray." Following the signs, Nick and I walked for a quarter of a mile or so to the bank of the river where Paul had gone to preach. There Paul and his companions had found a group of women, including a woman named Lydia from Thyatira (one of the Seven Cities of Revelation, which we had visited several years earlier) selling purple fabric from her hometown. After Paul preached to them, he baptized Lydia in the stream, and out of gratitude, Lydia invited Paul and the others into her house.

As we sat on the grassy bank of the river, Nick, ever the student of theology, pointed out that this was the ultimate example of the mustard seed: a couple of people prayed together with Paul, forming the first Christian church in Europe, and it spread its arms throughout the continent, ultimately dominating it and becoming the foundation of Western civilization and the most formidable institution in the history of man. "I could go on for an hour or more, in a theology class, or for twenty minutes in a sermon, about this very spot and the impact of what happened here had on the Christian world," Nick told me. "And in fact I have."

He pulled a pocket bible from his backpack, turned to the Book of Acts, and read.

> Jesus said, "The kingdom of God, or what parable shall we use for it? It is like a grain of mustard seed, which, when sown on the ground, is the smallest of all the seeds on earth, yet when it is sown it grows up and becomes larger than all the garden plants and puts out large branches, so that the birds of the air can make nests in its shade."

The Book of Acts, Nick explained, includes an interesting aside about Paul at Philippi: as he and his apostles were going to the river to pray they encountered a young slave girl, either demonically possessed or mentally disabled, whose babbling was interpreted as fortune-telling for a small fee paid to her owners—not uncommon in that part of the world. She began following Paul and his group about, declaring loudly that they were servants of God. Paul was sufficiently troubled by the performance that he commanded an evil spirit to come out of the girl. She was cured, but her owners, having lost their means of money-making, took Paul, Luke, and Timothy to the city authorities and demanded that Paul be punished. He was stripped, beaten and thrown into a dungeon with the others. But miraculously, a small earthquake knocked off the door of the cell. The guard, certain that he would be killed for releasing his prisoners, called out "Sirs, what must I do to be saved?" Paul told him to believe in Jesus Christ and baptized him—another addition to the new church at Philippi. After he was released, Paul went on his way, according to Acts, on foot along the Via Egnatia to Thessaloniki, about a hundred sixty kilometers to the West. Paul came back to Philippi several more times; first, in about 55 AD, seven years after his first visit, and after he had been imprisoned in Rome, when he wrote his letter to the Philippians, and three more times thereafter.

We found the small dungeon in some rocks where Paul was imprisoned (the door had never been repaired) although it was not marked in any way. But a guard, standing in a little hut nearby, told us that it was indeed where Paul had been held.

I was generally familiar with Paul's letter to the Philippians. I asked Nick, "So, from a theologian's perspective, is there anything unique about this letter, anything that distinguishes it from the others?" An interesting question, he said. We sat down on a wall overlooking the cave where Paul had been imprisoned. "It is his most joyful epistle," Nick said. "He loved Philippi. He had established a church, and found the people in Philippi to be particularly devoted to Christ. The Christians here were very fond of him." Paul wrote the letter about ten years or so after his last visit, while imprisoned, Nick said, but scholars are not sure where he was at the time. Nick suggested that we read some of that letter; he read chapter one aloud to me, and I read chapter two aloud to him.

St. Paul's Prison, Philippi, Greece

"When Paul would first come to a place like this," I asked Nick, "what was the reaction to what he was saying? What did people think about his teaching that Jesus was the Son of God, and was God? Was he considered as a serious scholar, a prophet, or just preaching another ideology or what?"

Nick replied that in most cases, Paul would travel with

an entourage of people, and word would go out well ahead of him—sometimes several days—that he was coming. "Obviously there was skepticism, and of course official Rome considered his teaching a threat to their power. But to many people, Paul's teaching was the most important thing they had ever heard." For the first time, Nick said, here was proof that there really was a god. God had appeared on earth as a human being—Jesus Christ. His teaching was convincing, and His crucifixion and resurrection proved His point, Nick explained. No longer did people need to wonder if what they believed was real. Now they had proof.

We talked about this at length. I thought about our many trips, the many places we had seen where Christianity had thrived in its early days, and how it was still a living faith, that people still believed it after so many years and so many attempts to prove it wrong. I thought about reading the Creed on that wall in Nicaea, talking to monks on Mt. Athos, in France, Romania, Syria, and Bulgaria who believed the same message with all their hearts and souls. All these trips, with that one conversation, seemed to fall into place. No longer were they just walking trips, bike trips, staying in cheap hotels, blisters and sore muscles and the rest. These had really been pilgrimages, and what I had seen and learned was a powerful message that had changed me, changed the way I thought about things, changed the way I would think for the rest of my life.

After several more hours of combing through the ruins, we drove on to Kavalla, the port town where Paul had landed, a few miles away. It no longer looked much like it must have to Paul; it was now a shabby and run-down port town, but with a few seaside restaurants and some low-brow beach houses and tourist homes. But, we discovered, the town did have friendly people. We went to several little hotels and B&Bs, all of which were full. At the last one, the owner told us to follow her in the car and led us a few blocks away to a private house. She jumped out and, in a minute, returned with the owner in tow, who said the whole house would be ours for the night for twenty euros. The owner, after a long chat about Kavala, went on her way to a neighbor's house, leaving her house and all her belongings to our care. We walked around much of the town before bed but found no evidence of St. Paul.

The next morning, we took a ferry to the little island of Thasos, just a few miles off shore from Kavalla. The northernmost Greek island, set well apart from the others, it was a sun-drenched place replete with white houses, resort hotels, and pizza shops. Nick had friends who had come here for several years for vacations. He mentioned that they had advised that he come here if he were anywhere in the vicinity. The island was well known, he told me, for little picturesque villages, sandy beaches, and crystal-clear water, and a lush, green and mountainous interior. "They called it the 'emerald of the Aegean,'" he told me.

We rented a couple of bicycles for the day and rode out along the coast road for several miles. White beach houses were scattered along sandy beaches which could have been on any coast around the Mediterranean or, for that matter, in the Caribbean. We stopped in a little café for a glass of beer, certainly the only English speakers, but in the midst of several Germans. I started up a conversation with a couple sitting at the next table (Germans always seem amazed when strangers start speaking to them). They were intrigued enough with an American who spoke German pretty well that the conversation continued, turning, before we were done, to the shattered

Greek economy and the fact that they, the Germans, were the ones who always seemed to bail out the Greeks. "We don't see many Americans here," one said. "What are you doing?" When I responded that we were on a pilgrimage, visiting places where Paul had been, they looked at me quizzically as if they were thinking, Paul who? German agnostics, I gathered.

We returned the bikes after several hours and walked up a steep hill behind where we found a square, probably built in the third century BC, complete with the ruins of temples, an acropolis and an amphitheater large enough to seat 3,000 people—still used for concerts and plays. On the way down, cut into the side of the cliff, we found one of the most famous points on Thasos—an image of the Greek god Pan, the god of nature and the wilds, carved into the rocks sometime well before Christ.

We took the return ferry to Kavalla, and then back to Thessaloniki airport—and from there, home again.

For the purposes of this account, at least, the trip along the via Egnatia would be the last and eleventh pilgrimage that Nick and I made together. Whether we'll take another remains to be seen. The first—the first chapter of this little book—was to Greece as well. A different region, to be sure, but one that had many connections to this one. So Greece was our first and our last, with many miles covered on foot, bicycles, trains, buses, boats, automobiles, horse-drawn wagons and, of course, airplanes to get there and back, with many sore muscles, many fascinating places visited, and countless conversations along the way.

As a last trip, the Via Egnatia was unique. It was, for me, an exhilarating combination of history, geopolitics, first class bicycling, and Christianity. Visiting places such as Athens, Thessaloniki, Pella, and Philippi along the Via Egnatia itself makes one realize how the Greeks and the Romans contributed to the world we live in today. Although I had seen many such places before, the concentration of these, so closely situated together, and their connections to other places we had visited on our pilgrimages, drew the world into a closer and more compact sphere. Geopolitics became a part of this pilgrimage because of the situation Greece found itself in politically. Virtually every conversation with a local would soon turn to the Greece's position vis-à-vis the European Union, its economic struggles, and its immigration crisis. And bicycling? Self-evident. Wonderful country roads, beautiful scenery, friendly people to point the way, and good food at the start and end of the day all added up to a trip that would be the envy of anyone who ever rode a bike for any distance.

As for Christianity, it was a thrill to travel along this road where the early Church had at least been partially developed, where some of the great biblical figures had travelled, preached and founded churches. Following in or close to the steps of Paul, reading his epistles, and discussing, with a knowledgeable friend, the part that he played in the great saga of the development and growth of the Christian church drives home what a formidable institution it is, how it has influenced Western civilization and Western thought, and the impact it has had on millions of lives, including my own.

Like all of these trips, the strongest impressions for me developed after I returned home, after I thought about the time there, the places visited and the people we met. Day to day, as one makes such a journey, the immediate thoughts are on finding the right road or path, or the sore muscles and blisters reminding us that we are not as young as we once were, or finding a place to stay and the rest of unplanned travel. But to weave it all together, to think of all the pieces that make such a journey is, for me, when I realize the value of such a trip in my beliefs, my thoughts and reminiscences. Even as I write this, ten months after returning from Thessaloniki, rarely a day goes by when some piece of the trip does not pop into my mind. It was more than a memorable trip—it was a truly life-changing pilgrimage.

Via Egnatia near Pella, Greece